Gamick (C000084810) ^

all the very
best from

Ranjit.

MP

RANJIT BOLT

Losing It A Novel In Verse

ILLUSTRATIONS BY RODDY MAUDE-ROXBY

Losing It by Ranjit Bolt
© Ranjit Bolt 2012

This edition published November 2012
by Muswell Press Ltd

First published in Great Britain in 2001 by John Murray
(Publishers)

Illustrations by Roddy Maude-Roxby

ISBN 978-0-9572136-6-1

Book design by Roelof Bakker

Printed by Shortrun Press Ltd

 www.muswell-press.co.uk

In Memoriam, Sydney Bolt
1920-2012

ONE

I thought I'd start by bringing in
My beautiful young heroine –
Lucy, as lovely as the day
Is long, or almost, anyway.
And yet, for all her loveliness,
She had to suffer the distress,
With twenty less than two years off,
Of being the mock, the jeer, the scoff
Of all her friends and peers, because,
Not mincing words with you, she was,
At eighteen – don't be shocked at this –
As virginal as Artemis!
And whereas, long ago, Lord knows –
In Homer's time, or Cicero's
Or many ages I could name,
So far from being a cause of shame,
Such purity was highly prized,
Virginity being recognised
As a most honourable state,
Today a girl must get a mate,
And if she lets the time slip by
Without one, people wonder why,
The taunts and brickbats start to fly.
In these lewd times, virginity
Is practically a stigma we
Wear more reluctantly each day
After the age of – sixteen, say.
        Instinctively, young Lucy knew
A pretty-boy would scarcely do –

She snubbed them time and time again –
She *must* have someone with a brain.
She was, herself, no quarter-wit
(In fact, the total opposite)
And would prefer a clever fellow,
Be he as plain as straw is yellow,
To someone dull, or dim, or dumb,
Although as handsome as they come.
How right she was! There's nothing worse
Than being unable to converse
On equal terms with someone who
You've picked to share a bed with you.
It breaks your heart when, after all
The night's cavorting, they let fall,
Over the eggs, or muesli, stray
Remarks, opinions, that betray
A total want of intellect –
Romantic fantasies are wrecked
And, as the grisly meal drags on,
You're *praying* for them to be gone.

　　She'd had, for three years now, or more,
Good-looking morons by the score
Pursuing her – they were a bore.
But, strange to say, she hadn't met
A bright boy she could fancy yet.
Some had been ugly and not quite
Proportionately erudite,
While others looked quite cute, and were
Smart – but not smart enough for her.
The search was profitless and long.
Sometimes she almost got it wrong –
Thought she had found the perfect person

In fact could not have picked a worse one
Was ready to perform the act,
Or nearly, but escaped intact.
And so, as three years came and went,
She'd stayed in her predicament,
Just like a sweet, unwritten tune
That hoped to be composed quite soon.
     Virginity, my curse on you!
What dire lengths I was driven to
To shake you off in my own youth!
You drove me mad, and that's the truth!
And then it happened, quite by chance
All gone were shame, and ignorance
As, man instead of bashful boy,
Heart flooded with conceit and joy,
I ran round Oxford screaming out
The news, lest there be any doubt,
Dismaying friends, naming the girl,
And startling tourists in the Turl.
     As spots to get deflowered in go
London's the likeliest one I know
And there it was that Lucy hied.
Her great-aunt happened to reside
Near Hampstead Heath, and she had said
That Lucy could have board and bed
For just as long as she might need
To do the necessary deed.
Her parents worried, but agreed
(If they had tried to thwart her aim
She would have set off all the same)
But yes, they fretted. Who would not?
Lucy in London – that fleshpot!

That hydra, readying its maw
To swallow their sweet daughter raw!
And was she raw! – completely green –
Despite being nubile, and nineteen,
And born in an anarchic age
When teenage pregnancy's the rage.
Her friends were all ahead of her
And that was the most poignant spur
To Lucy's urgent quest: peer groups,
While best shrugged off as nincompoops,
Are never easily dismissed –
It takes real gumption to resist
The constant pleasure they apply.
Her parents knew this, which was why
They didn't stand in Lucy's way
Though they were deeply troubled, nay
Distraught.
      Within a day or two
A cab climbed Fitzjohn's Avenue
With Lucy in the back. "So this
Is it! The great metropolis!"
She murmured. "I've a shrewd idea
I'm going to rather like it here."
Mind you, the place she'd picked to live
Was hardly representative:
Hampstead, which roosts high up above
The city, like a Georgian dove,
With more quaint nooks and strange dead ends
Than teenage girls have Facebook friends.
Its narrow, ancient streets, its squares,
Bankers' retreats and luvvies' lairs,
Many regard as rather twee

While still allowing this to be
A beautiful and charming spot.
"Was it Well Road, then, luv, or what?
Coz if it was, we're bleedin' 'ere,"
The cabbie growled, then gave a leer,
For all he'd had a rotten day,
And added: "You care now, eh?
There's lotsa dodgy blokes out there."
Then gawped as he discharged his fare,
For he, if anyone, would know
That figures such as hers don't grow
On trees. He watched this living ray
Of vernal sunshine walk away,
In his wing mirror for a while,
The day's best looker, by a mile.

     Her aunt's house was a Gothic pile
Close, as I said, to Hampstead Heath.
It made beholders catch their breath,
If they had any taste at all,
For it was cut out to appal,
Quite perfect in its hideousness
You'd shy away from it, unless
You are the type that can enthuse
About redundant curlicues,
Arches that make no visual sense
And other such embellishments,
Which covered it, and which belong
To the New Gothic style gone wrong.
In short, this mansion was a mess
(Though quite imposing, nonetheless).

     She pulled the bell-pull, and a weird,
Lugubrious butler soon appeared,

Got up in garb of dismal black
More suited to a century back
Than any menial of today.
His manner suited his array –
Silent, and solemn as the tomb,
He ushered Lucy to her room.
"Dinner will be at eight," said he,
Then turned about decrepitly
And slowly sidled off.
"Queer sort!
Quite scary house, too," Lucy thought,
"I wonder if I've boobed? Ah well,
Stay positive – too soon to tell –
You pull yourself together, girl –
We're damned well giving this a whirl!"
By chivvying herself this way
She kept anxiety at bay
Till it was suddenly dispelled
When, wafting through the house, she smelled
The marvellous, savoury yet sweet
Aroma of some roasting meat
And fear gave way to appetite.
     At table they were three that night -
Unless you count the jet black cat
That, through the evening, mutely sat
On Aunt Alicia's ancient knee.
"So here you are, my dear!" cried she
Lolling, contented, in her chair
And smiling with a wicked air.
She wrapped her great black woollen shawl
About her, and tipped back the tall,
Black, pointed hat upon her head

While, with the gaze of the undead,
She scrutinized her lovely niece.
"Algernon, pass the brandy, please!"
How typical the old witch looked –
Eyes brightly twinkling, nose hooked,
While kindness, in her gaze, was blent
With something more malevolent.
Much, to be frank, was pretty strange
About her ménage. Its mélange
Of things and people who'd just slipped
Out of a Hammer Horror script:
Her butler, not to badmouth him,
Seemed, if not evil, somewhat grim,
Added to which, the mansion where
This quite grotesque and gruesome pair
Hung out, posed questions by the score:
Scuttling footsteps scraped each floor,
You couldn't name one feature which
Was not replete with Gothic kitsch –
The goggling gargoyles standing guard
Over the horrible façade;
Long, lamp-lit passages that creaked,
Which rats patrolled, while barn-owls shrieked
Out in the grounds, and night-jars whirred;
Poltergeists, too, must be inferred –
Though nothing had quite moved as yet
Various objects seemed to fret
About their stationery state
And whisper: "We've not long to wait –
Just sit this silly supper out
And, brother, how we'll shift about!"
        But to my tale: Alicia had,

Some couplets back, addressed a lad
Whose age was more or less the same
As Lucy's – Algernon by name,
He being her grandson, and in truth
As weird and off-the-wall a youth
As she a crone. He sat beside
His cousin, yet he hadn't tried
To start a conversation – no,
Completely mum he was, as though
Deaf, dumb and blind, so unaware
He seemed that she was sitting there.
This baffled Lucy. All night long
He shunned her like a nasty pong,
She'd never been so dissed, so scorned –
She ventured a remark, he yawned
And seemed to wish she'd venture none,
As though he might have had more fun.
In Purgatory.
It's often true
That if we're paid attention to
By someone of the opposite
Gender, we're not impressed one bit,
But if we're shown no earthly heed
A sudden, quite compelling need
Will soon start forming in our head
To get that person into bed.
That was how Lucy felt tonight:
He was no babe, but he was bright,
Nay, *burned* with intellectual fire
And that's a licence to look dire,
Or certain women deem it so,
Lucy being one such, as we know.

A dazzling, cerebral flow
He kept up. He was plain, all right,
A truly horrifying sight,
The inverse of an oil-painting –
His eyes, his nose, his everything
Instead of going in, stuck out,
Or else the other way about:
His belly swelled, his arse caved in;
Low-browed he was, with sallow skin;
His teeth were riven by many a gat;
Legs long and thin, arms short and fat;
Eyes shrunk by bottle-bottom specs –
A walking antidote to sex
He seemed. Yet from his thick lips came,
On any theme you cared to name,
So much, and all so apposite,
And interlaced with charm and wit
That Lucy pardoned the disgrace,
The *nightmare* of his form, and face.
How lucid his opinions were!
To what a range did he refer
Of learned sources to support
Each judgement, each arresting thought
And scintillating aperçu.
But Lucy might, for all he knew,
Or seemed in the least bit to care,
Have been a table or a chair -
Alicia only he addressed
From start to finish, and caressed
With talk of literature and art,
The whole of which he knew by heart,
And *on* it had a trenchant view,

With politics and finance too,
History, philosophy, music, food,
And yet on none he seemed a pseud.
He was as well-read as they come –
As well as Voltaire, and then some –
Sweet Jesus, was he erudite –
He'd read all day, he'd read all night,
Read till his eyes yelled: "Look, you creep,
Stop reading! Get some sodding sleep!"
So Lucy guessed – correctly, too.
     When midnight came, and they withdrew,
She had been pierced through with the pain
Of Algernon's complete disdain.
She made her way upstairs to bed
Inwardly fuming, seeing red,
Resolved to show this dweeb, this swot
Just who was who, and what was what,
By bedding him, without delay.
Despite a quite exhausting day
She kissed goodbye to that night's rest,
Was angry, lustful, and depressed.
At two a.m. her self-esteem
Still harped upon a single theme -
Fed up of waiting one more hour
To net him, and assert her power,
She left her room and off she crept
To find the one in which he slept.
Down creaking passages she went
With wild, lascivious intent
Till, at the end of one, she saw
A line of light beneath a door
And knew instinctively, at once,

That this room must be Algernon's.
"I mean, who else's could it be?
A little geek like that," thought she,
"Scattering learned quotes around,
He's studying something, I'll be bound.
Given the vast amount he knows
It's reasonable to suppose
He never sleeps, just reads and reads –
God save us from such bookish weeds!"
Thus Lucy fumed in her denial,
Wanting him madly all the while.
    She knocked. No sound. So why the light?
"Sleeps with it on? I guess he might…"
Na – studying, the little nerd."
Listening more carefully, she heard
The sound of fingers tapping keys –
"He's writing something, if you please!"
She knocked a second time. "Come in!"
She entered, and was facing him,
She in her skimpy negligée,
He eying her, as if to say –
Well, something cutting, anyway.
He went on typing, which was rude
And, given so much pulchritude,
So lightly clad, at two a.m.,
Suggested an excess of phlegm
To say the least. He wasn't dim -
A young girl was disturbing him,
Not *any* girl, but cute as pie,
At this late hour, he must know why,
Yet he did nothing, typed away
As if her legs weren't on display,

Her lovely long white arms all bare,
And shoulders, under auburn hair.
    "Algernon? Still awake?" said she.
"What's that you're working on? Tell me…
Some masterpiece?" "It's… nothing much –
A novel… that is, not as such…
Call it a kind of overview –
My *take* on where we are, and who.
Well, now he'd talked to her at least –
Tacit hostilities had ceased
And that was something – not enough
But something. "Oh, it's sorry stuff,
Dear cousin – just you wait and see –
No one'll publish it," said he,
But I'm incredibly behind
So, Lucy, if you wouldn't mind…"
    He went to work, she went away
Having done nothing to allay
Her pain, and even more impressed
With Algie, for she little guessed
That all North London, new to her,
Is basically just one big whir
Of diverse up-to-date machines
All churning chapters out, or scenes –
We just can't help it, it's a bug,
It ought to get us thrown in jug
But it's as natural to our class
As to eat, sleep, or wipe one's arse.
When the North London evenings come
Just listen, and you'll hear the hum
Of writers, droning on like bees
On laptops, iPads, and PCs.

Nature's soft nurse (that's sleep, of course)
Soothed Lucy's woes at last, perforce.
And even Algie's pattering keys
Did have the decency to cease.
Later, the rosy Hampstead dawn
Woke on the Heath and, with a yawn,
Sensing it was too soon to break,
Pulled up the misty sheets to take
Another forty winks before
She gave the signal for the roar
Of London life to recommence.
From her nocturnal devilments
The witch returned. Each night she flew
Off on her magic broom, to brew
Fresh mischief up. But even she,
A votaress of Hecatë,
Was a tad weary, and could use
A reinvigorating snooze.

The butler, rested and awake,
As always, just before daybreak,
Tested his tardy, ancient legs.
Prior to preparing bacon, eggs,
Toast, coffee, for which all would ask,
His long day's first, lugubrious task,
He brooded in the bluish-grey
Final ten minutes before day.

TWO

Lucy awoke, her stomach sank,
She shuddered inwardly and shrank
From the sheer shame of what she'd done.
"I mean, to try to bed someone
 I'd only met six hours before!
Go creeping down the corridor
And knock him up, and… oh, my God!
Why did I meet the little sod?
He's clever, *brilliant* – that's for sure,
But *sexually* he's immature,
He must be – it's as plain as day –
He spurned me – in my negligée!
I must adjust my first idea –
I've focused far too much, I fear,
On abstract, naked intellect –
Men are like wood in this respect –
Unseasoned timbers aren't much use:
From last night's failure, I deduce:
I need a bloke who's lived a bit,
Is *weathered, wise,* and has the wit,
When girls drop in at two a.m.,
To know what one should do with them!"
Lost in these thoughts, downstairs she went
For matutinal nourishment.
        Thank **** for breakfast! When the day
Is getting grimly underway
And fear, futility, despair
Are hovering in the morning air,
I feel I can't proceed, am sick

Of life… and then they work their trick –
Eggs, bacon, toast, jam, coffee, tea –
When their sweet smells waft up to me
I feel I can resume the fight –
Courage and hope are not gone – quite.
　　Lucy, of course, being young and blithe,
Thought it was fun to be alive –
She had no sick, hurt mind to heal –
Breakfast, for her, was just a meal.
She ate a hearty one, at that,
Then brushed her teeth, donned coat and hat
And went exploring, gaily strode
Through Belsize Park, down Chalk Farm Road
To Camden. Here you start to feel
The bijou, bourgeois paintwork peel,
A touch of sleaze is in the air,
Half naked Goths are everywhere
And foreigners in wild pursuit
Of tat – expensive tat, to boot.
In half an hour she reached the Lock
Where instant major culture shock
Awaited her, a small-town girl
Confronted with the city's whirl
For the first time. The Lock in Spring,
Gradually reawakening
After its winter sleep, becomes
A tourist trap that fairly hums
With tawdry life – an inferno
(At weekends frighteningly so)
Of people, junk, and atmosphere,
Its purpose not entirely clear,
In essence tacky, and yet not

A wholly unappealing spot —
At least, it's charming when the sun
Turns the canal (as it had done
Today) into a sheet of gold
And warms the gaily painted old
Decrepit houses built about
The waterway, their walls decked out
In pastel shades — blues, yellows, pinks -
"Romantic, this!" the stranger thinks,
And so it is. But, Lord, the *stalls* —
How it bewilders and appals,
That mass of tasteless merchandise,
As hard on wallets as on eyes,
While the crowds passing to and fro
In almost a *cloacal* flow
Disgust one, as they mill along,
With their bad manners, and their pong.
      She bought a leather mini and,
Spotting a café close at hand,
Sat with a cappuccino there
Out in the early April air.
An hour had more or less gone by
When a hunched figure caught her eye.
He squatted on a shelf, or ledge,
Just inches from the water's edge
Fixing its surface with a stare
Of deep, of absolute despair,
Like someone with a dire intent...
Then Lucy blinked, and in he went!
Into the water, with a plop!
Her jaw had barely time to drop -
She took a second, less, to doff

Her coat, or rather, fling it off,
Then in she plunged straight after him.
It wasn't that he couldn't swim,
He seemed to let himself sink down,
Without a cry, *resolved* to drown.
Quite limp he was, from feeling low,
He didn't thrash around, and so
Lucy soon had her hands about
His underarms, and hauled him out.
　　It wasn't in the least that he'd
Solicited this noble deed
And now he sat there on the bank,
No happier, and a deal more dank,
Uttering no thanks for being restored
To an existence he abhorred –
He wasn't angry, merely sad:
So he was still alive? Too bad.
She watched him, trying to fathom why
He, *anyone*, would want to die
And, watching *her* in turn, he took
His cue from her enquiring look –
His face contorted with malaise,
He barely found the strength to raise
His shoulders in a mournful shrug,
Then spoke: "If love of life's a bug
I haven't caught it yet. My bit
Of Life's great jigsaw doesn't fit –
I fail to see the *point* – unless,
Of course, the point is pointlessness."
"But even so, to want to *die!*"
She cried. He looked her in the eye
Then at the rest of her as well

And maybe – Lucy couldn't tell –
His face did brighten just a tad.
He would have had to have been mad
Not to have cheered up at the sight
Of something Nature'd got so right -
"Perhaps I ought to think again…"
He mused.

      Young nymphs *can* furnish men
In middle age, of maudlin cast
With cheering echoes of the past,
Reviving one last, lingering spark
Where all had seemed quite cold, and dark.
She'd saved him, had this sweet young thing –
He couldn't help imagining
Implausible scenarios
In which she soothed away his woes,
Removed him from his wretched state -
The *Hell* in which he'd lived of late…
She seemed to like him… He was sly,
Knew every wherefore, every why
Of women, and the mating game -
Out from his filing system came
The card to fit this specimen…
"Well, cheers, if we don't meet again,
Have a great life, and all that crap,
May what you seek land in your lap,
But now it's thank you, and goodbye…
My flat's just there – I'd best get dry."
"I'm coming with you!" Lucy said,
"You can't escape me, I'm afraid,
Who knows what stunt you might pull next!"
So, with a show of being vexed,

Though this was what he'd angled for,
He let her walk him to his door –
Then come in for a glass of wine –
Then have another, which was fine
And merely part of making friends,
But they had rounded several bends
When, feeling that his dangerous fit
Was over, or the worst of it,
She finally got up to go.
Then, since she brought, in doing so,
Her body close to his somehow,
He caught her on the rise, and now,
Half up, half down, and face to face,
They fell into a long embrace.
Just that, though, an embrace, no more,
And no less than she'd bargained for,
But quite enough to cook her goose -
Resistance would have been no use –
Love had just downed her, like a snipe.
For, conversely, there is a type
Of melancholy Romeo
Aged fifty, forty-five, or so,
Who can attract a certain kind
Of young girl, partly with his mind
Partly for Freudian reasons that
I scarcely think worth hinting at,
So, leaving those aside, it looked
As though our heroine was hooked.
      One thing he said I should report:
Lucy expressed the following thought:
"A *woman's* what you need," she said,
"Another presence in your bed –

What the *Symposium* calls a 'half,'"
She added with a nervous laugh,
Afraid she'd waxed too erudite.
She could have kissed that fear goodnight –
He'd read his Plato and much more
Here was no cute young brainless bore.
"A wife, for instance…" she went on,
"That is to say… er… have you one?
I see no ring…" – "I live alone.
I *had* a wife a long while back –
A witch – a nymphomaniac
Who came and cast her spell on me
(And I mean that quite literally)."
"You're saying…?" "That she was a *mage*,
A sorceress, who'd concealed her age,
Made herself young again, with spells.
It's not the sort of tale one tells
And you'll suspect me, now it's told,
Of being a freak… eight centuries old
She was, but looked as young as you –
A teenage girl – and gorgeous, too.
Then, one fine day, don't ask me why –
Either from spite, one in the eye,
Or else sheer whimsy, just to see –
To have some fun, by fazing me –
She made herself grow *old* again –
She spoke some spell, or didn't when
She should have done, and turned into
A hag once more… Don't laugh! It's true!
The magic wore off overnight,
I woke to an atrocious sight:
Beside me in the bed there lay

An ancient, wrinkled, hideous fay."
"What did you do?" – "What did I do?
I left. I felt entitled to.
She took it badly, which was rich –
She hadn't *said* she was a witch,
Still less that she was so damned *old* –
Facts she'd no business to withhold
But which I only learned the day
Her youthful coating peeled away.
Yet she resented my response
And, when I did a bunk at once,
Wrote to me, railing, sounding pained –
I was the traitor, she maintained –
A fickle, superficial swine.
She had the *cheek* to take that line!
What right had she to rant and moan?
She'd *hoodwinked* me, the sly old crone!
Well, since then, I've been on my own –
I'm well past my romantic prime -
Women pass through from time to time -
They only flatter to deceive –
As fast as they arrive they leave -
Nor am I keen for them to stay."
"The witch has cursed you!" – "I dare say."

    The spirit of love is quick and fresh
And now held Lucy in its mesh.
Whole hours she wasted wondering
When the infernal phone would ring
With *his* voice on the other end –
The waiting drove her round the bend.
(His name was Richard, by the way.)
So she grew more and more *distrait*

If not downright obsessional...
"I fished him out of a canal,
I kissed him in his flat – so what?
That's no excuse to lose the plot!"
All day she would reiterate
And din these words into her pate
In an attempt to ease her pain –
The trouble was, she'd gone insane,
She'd given absolute control -
Handed the latchkey to her soul
To somebody she hardly knew.
Love does that – it can stage a coup –
Depose our wits, and carry on
Till all our strength of will has gone,
Whipping us up like a meringue...
It whipped, and whipped, and then he rang...
         After the agonising wait
She now began to palpitate,
Her breath came panicky and short,
To his remarks she could retort
Only with gushing gibberish.
He sensed that he had hooked his fish
His grasp of the seducer's art,
Plus, possibly, his age, in part,
His sadness, too – a heady mix
Quite as effective as sly tricks -
Had won her over.
He was sure
She *liked* his being so mature,
The opposite of some young pup,
He played these various aspects up,
Was *weary* in his style, and tone

And worldly wise, as if he'd known
All that there was worthwhile to know
Since... ooh... a century ago.
Soon she was eating from his palm
So unremitting was his charm.
Now she could eat again, and sleep,
And chafe at being in so deep,
Passion and pride complexly mixed,
Until at length a date was fixed:
They were to dine *à quatre, chez elle.*

    I dare say it was just as well
That Lucy should, on their first night,
Be spared romance and candlelight –
Being new to this, she didn't need
The tension such occasions breed.
The witch, on whom she had relied
To green-light things, was got onside.
"A man? Delightful, dear! Well played!
Your dismal demons shall be laid
To rest at last! And have no fear
About... *concluding matters* here –
I'm scarcely what you'd call a prude -
Provided that you don't intrude
Upon my peace with noxious noise,
Remaining *muted* in your joys,
I grant you a complete free hand –
I give you leave, nay, I *demand*
That you secure your cherry's loss,
Shake off the awful albatross
That's hanging round your nubile neck –
Was *I,* at your age? Was I heck!"
    I understand that silence clause,

I know why noises gave her pause:
Few things disturb the psyche more
Than hearing, from an upper floor,
Or lower, or the room next door,
The grunt and groan, the thump and thud
Of sex. You feel, oh, such a *dud*
Hearing them at it through the night
While you, like some hermaphrodite
Or old maid, lie there, on your tod,
The odd man out, and none so odd,
Harmlessly, hopelessly tucked up
With a George Eliot, and a cup
Of unerotic Ovaltine,
Imagining the steamy scene
Being played below, or overhead,
Or right behind you, as I said.
     The awesome hour was near, it seemed –
No wonder that night Lucy dreamed
Of cherries being plucked from trees
And ritual obscenities
Enacted at her aunt's behest –
The girl was revved up – *and* the rest.

THREE

Now, it's a fact that many a date
Has hinged on what the couple ate.
(*And* drank, of course – in fact, today,
But for a case of Cabernet,
I might myself be single still –
That, and a morning after pill
That didn't work.) So, to enhance
Lucy's own charms, the best of aunts
Laid on the kind of cracking feast
By which the wheels of love are greased.
The butler doubled as the cook
And, under strict instructions, took
Especially elaborate care.
Alicia'd bidden him prepare
A lemon tart to murder for
And now the *lobster thermidor*
And *boeuf en daube* he'd also planned
Were taking shape beneath his hand.
      Upstairs, while studious Algernon
Went tying and amending on
Lucy was titivating, less
Than certain as to choice of dress,
Colour of lipstick, and the like,
But confident that she could strike
A telling, if not killer blow
And nab her aging Romeo.
Garments galore she donned, then dumped,
Until eventually she plumped
For something slinky, velvet, black,

Armless, and plunging at the back,
That, if she wished, could slyly rise
To show her shapely, snow-white thighs,
Or else, if feeling insecure,
Stay down and make her look demure.
   The witch was whimsical – although
She'd undertaken not to go
Off on her nightly escapade
And ply her necromantic trade
But stay and act as chaperone
By eight o'clock, away she'd gone
Leaving, for back-up, Algernon,
But he was in a purple spell,
His book was going very well
And naturally he didn't feel
Like downing tools to eat a meal,
Which meant that, after all, there'd be
Just him and her (or he and she).
   Not one to make a lady wait
He turned up on the dot of eight,
That being the time that they'd agreed.
At first she was a touch weak-kneed
But soon he'd put her quite at ease
With artful, winsome pleasantries
That went straight to her head like wine –
In no time things were going fine –
Under the candelabra's glow
My, did the conversation flow,
The lobster, with a fine Sancerre,
Broke down all walls between the pair;
He talked, she laughed, the beef was brought,
She talked, more loudly than she ought

Thanks to the wine, but what of that?
She'd got him, or she'd eat her hat.
(Of Aunt Alicia she said nought -
She thought – I don't know what she thought –
No reason he should find it odd –
He'd been a witch's *spouse*, poor sod,
And had a torrid time with her,
Or so he'd led her to infer
That day in Camden – anyhow
She left Alicia out for now.)
    Having feared sinking like a stone
Now she was glad that she'd been thrown
In at the deep end, quite alone…
A Château Margaux past compare
Soon went the way of the Sancerre;
By the Sauterne and lemon tart
Each one had won the other's heart
And was already dropping hints.
What need of coffee, or of mints?
Or of liqueurs, or port, or cheese?
This was a moment they must seize…
They were upstairs, and in the sack
When Aunt Alicia got back…
Lucy, although already tossed
On waves of pleasure, hadn't lost
Her hated cherry – not quite yet –
But things were certainly well set.
    The canny and percipient witch
Guessed all had gone without a hitch –
The aphrodisiac in the wine
Had worked, it did so every time –
Ground aconite and hellebore.

"My great-niece is about to score,
Add to the endless pile of pairs,"
She muttered, as she went upstairs,
Her forehead furrowed by a frown,
And, doffing pointed hat and gown,
Lay down to rest. But then a whim
Seized her, to take a look at him,
This Don Juan, who'd at last succeeded
Where scores had failed. What was it he did
That others failed to? "Yes, what knack
Does *he* have, that the rest all lack?
Nah! It's some twerp with a cute face,"
She changed her tack, "how commonplace."

She crept along a corridor,
Peeped into Lucy's room, and saw…
A body, face, a *man* she knew!
Richard, it was! The Richard who,
Decades ago had been her spouse,
Before he'd buggered off, the louse!
Yes, it was him, as plain as day!
She *reeled* with fury and dismay,
Rejection, anguish, raged anew –
She knew just what she had to do…
She softly crept into the room –
Through mullioned windows, a full moon
Lit up his naked, hated form –
In quite good shape he was, the worm –
Time hadn't taken quite the toll
It does on men's bods, on the whole:
His stomach, down the years, had not
Puffed out into the usual pot,
His limbs were lithe and sinewy.

He saw her. Stunned, instinctively
He moved a hand to hide his cock
While staring, like a hare in shock,
At his ex-wife.
As Congreve said:
"Hell Hath no fury…" She saw red.
Lord, how she scowled, and howled, and swore
Vengeance as dire as none before.
He acted cool and unafraid:
"Hello, Alicia," he said,
"How's tricks? But, really, please chill out –
What call is there to scream and shout?"

     Lucy, throughout this little scene,
Was working out what it might mean.
They knew each other, that was clear,
But where from? She had no idea.
And what had got her great-aunt's goat?
But then the beldame cleared her throat
And thus began: "A pretty sight!
My word, you look the part, all right!
Man: nut-brown, wiry and mature,
Girl, oh so pretty, sweet and pure
And fondling one another's bum –
As cool a couple as they come!
Couples!" she roared, "I *loathe* the breed!
Life – mine, for instance – would proceed
Better without them, by a mile,
There's something syrupy and vile
About the whole revolting crew!
My modest pleasures (precious few
In view of my advanced decay)
Are *spoiled* by couples every day!

I might be in a restaurant –
A quiet supper's all I want -
I'm sitting in my usual nook
Perusing some improving book
Feeling that life is not so dire
Nor solitude *that* deep a mire,
What with a book, good wine, nice food -
A strong and stoic attitude -
When in will walk a blissful pair
Of lovers, whose complacent air,
Hand-holding, smooching, squeaks of joy,
Make me quite nauseous, and destroy
All my composure, so hard-won,
With their disgusting carrying-on.
        Or I'm outside in some café
Whiling the pleasant time away,
Happily watching life go by,
When suddenly there'll catch my eye
A couple, strolling down the street,
All lovey-dovey, candy-sweet,
Gazing into each other's eyes
And holding hands, and rubbing thighs
Till my gorge rises at the sight
And my contented mood takes flight!
It happens everywhere I go,
No spell can stop it, that I know,
For magic's very hit or miss,
But on your strawberries I *shall* piss!"
        With these grim words she raised her hand,
Too mad to go and fetch her wand,
Looking sublimely fierce and fell,
And spoke a devastating spell...

It didn't happen straightaway -
For a short while he seemed OK –
But actually, by slow degrees,
Was shrinking. As one sometimes sees,
During the period of twilight,
At first no change, then very slight,
Then, as if someone pulled a switch,
Night's fallen, all is black as pitch,
So Lucy, looking at her mate,
First had no inkling of his fate,
Then, in a ghastly moment, knew
What he was being turned into…
He shrank, grew great long ears, and fur –
There, nuzzling sadly up to her,
His head ten inches from the floor,
A *hare* now squatted, where before
The lover of her dreams had been.
She gazed upon this desolate scene
And mourned for love turned sour, and wept
To think her cherry had been kept
So narrowly, against her wish,
When she had hooked a decent fish
At last, but that was life, she guessed,
And it was pointless to protest.
      "There, there, dear!" Aunt Alicia said,
Patting the girl's despondent head,
"There's plenty more fish in the sea
And you'll net lots, believe you me,
Tons of 'em, if you're so inclined,
Container-loads, if you've a mind."
With these, and suchlike words, the old
Wise crone encouraged and cajoled,

Repeating, in a different guise
Each time, the same familiar, wise
And soothing saw, till Lucy's eyes
Grew heavy, and began to close.

    The hare looked up and twitched his nose,
He seemed both puzzled and distressed.
Deciding that it might be best
To get him quickly cracking at
His newfound natural habitat,
Alicia grabbed the bell and rang
And, in a trice, her serving man
Had carted off the hapless beast.
Quite sensibly, it was released
On Hampstead Heath – though hares may not
Frequent it, rabbits love the spot.
Here Richard tried out being a hare –
Stood on his hind legs, boxed the air,
Cried madly to the April moon
And was experiencing soon
A strange new, hybrid consciousness,
As hare grew more, and man grew less -
Part human, racked by angst and doubt,
Part hare, with zilch to fret about
Apart from staying alive, maybe.

    Lucy awoke at ten to three
With an excruciating start -
The sure sign of a broken heart.
At once, instinctively, she knew,
As troubled sleepers often do,
That she would not doze off again.
She rose and, through a leaded pane,
Surveyed a Heath all ghostly white

And eerie in the full moon's light,
And thought, with sadness, of the hare
Spending its first, cold night out there.
"Life can be very cruel," she sighed,
Then, in the garden, she descried…
She couldn't credit what she'd seen…
"Algernon!" No! It can't have been.
"I'm seeing things. It's stress," she thought.
But it was nothing of the sort —
There in the garden, down below,
The surreptitious so-and-so,
Off on some dodgy escapade,
Was Algie, carrying a spade!

FOUR

She tailed him, as would you or I –
It's nothing to be baffled by:
How often does adventure prove
A cure for disappointed love.
She crossed, first Well, then East Heath Road,
A hundred yards ahead, he strode
Between the first and second pond,
Then up the rising path beyond
That takes you on to Parliament Hill.
At length he stopped, and with a will
Began to dig, to throw up earth
As if he hoped to get to Perth
By morning – flung it up, he did,
With furious zest, while Lucy hid
Behind a nearby poplar tree
And watched him fascinatedly,
Uncertain how she should proceed
But very curious indeed.
         The Heath was at its haunted best –
A perfect moon, a landscape blessed
With Nature's beauties and with Art's
Mixed in superb, unequal parts:
The brooding, vast expanse, with here
A dark copse, giving an idea
Of something sinister, the hoot
Of the odd owl just adding to it,
And there a sleeping pond, now lit
By such a moon as silvered it
And gave it a disturbing sheen.

Forming a backdrop to the scene,
Dormant, as Lucy looked, and still,
Right opposite, rose Highgate Hill,
It's darkly wooded slopes, up which
Clamber the houses of the rich,
Like blocks of firewood on a pyre,
Saint Michael's pseudo-Gothic spire
Sitting atop it. This, tonight,
The moon had turned a ghostly white,
It gleamed there, spectral, graceful, high,
A great stone needle with no eye.
Such were the sights that Lucy saw,
Was taking in with quiet awe –
A scene replete with English charm, a
Painting by Constable, or Palmer,
Come magically to life.
A mug
Of tea (or soup?) then on he dug.
Lucy, whose free and feisty soul
Rejected any passive role,
Was wearying of watching. She
Stepped boldly from behind her tree
And hailed him: "Algernon! Hello!
You're a mysterious so-and-so!
What's all the manic digging for?"

   Algie began to hum and haw
And didn't answer. Lucy pressed
Till he eventually confessed
(Half of him longed to anyway)
What had occurred the previous day:
Browsing he'd been, in Fawkes' bookshop
"When what do you suppose should drop

Out of a copy of Marvell?
A treasure map! I couldn't tell
Which spot it was referring to –
That it was somewhere here, I knew –
The thing was headed "HEATH", you see,
And, well, what other could it be
Fawkes being a Hampstead shop and all -
(It's in Flask Walk, if you recall).
This splodge, and that one at the top's
Supposed to indicate a copse
And, this being quite a wooded part,
It seemed a likely place to start –
Now tell me I'm a nincompoop.
You must be freezing. Have some soup."
He handed her his thermos, she
Was drinking from it thirstily
When suddenly they heard a sound,
A horse's neigh, and, turning round,
Found themselves staring wildly at
A man in a three-cornered hat,
Swathed in a cloak, astride a horse,
Pistol in hand (it was, of course,
Dick Turpin, Hampstead denizen,
Hero, and prince of highwaymen.)
       The spectre chilled them to the core.
"I wonder what you're lookin' for!
Could it be treasure?" cried Turpin,
His face split open in a grin,
"No need to answer, 'coz you are.
'ad any luck, then, boy, so far?
No? Well, I didn't think you 'ad.
It's no use askin' *me*, me lad,

I's clean forgotten where I 'id it –
'Twas all the damned Madeira did it –
Me wits is fuddled up, right through.
I'd stop for now, if I was you,
You're clean wore out, or oughter be –
You come 'n 'ave a drink wi' me,
And bring yer lass 'ere, if ye choose,
'Twill warm ye, will a bit o' booze.
Well? 'Ow's about it?"
"Why not?"
"Fine!"
Though it was well past closing time
They sensed that any argument
Would not be wise, so off they went.
Turpin put Lucy on Black Bess
And then, as if they couldn't guess,
He added, with a graceful bow:
"Dick Turpin. 'Oo might *you* be, now?"
    If all acquaintanceships begin
With parties feeling their way in
In this case it was doubly so,
Dick having *died* some time ago.
This man was either, in effect, a
Mental defective, or a spectre.
They half believed, half doubted him
Until they reached the Spaniards Inn
And, issuing from it, heard the din
Of drunken, phantom raucousness.
Dick quickly tethered up Black Bess
And, trepidation to the fore,
They ventured with him through the door.
    A lively place, as ghost inns went,

This was – a Georgian ferment
Of drunkards, gamesters, footpads, whores,
Hacks, lawyers, quaffing without pause,
Dressed à la circa seventeen thirty,
Some talk politics, some dirty,
Caressing rumps and loosening stays,
Conversing, just like nowadays,
The only way such dives allow,
In yells, to beat the general row.
        Dick bagged his corner of the snug,
A buxom barmaid brought a jug
Of foaming ale for Algernon,
A bottle, an enormous one,
Of the Madeira Dick preferred,
While Lucy didn't breathe a word
About her usual (rum and coke)
But tried the wine, which made her choke.
A comely serving wench came by
And Turpin slapped a giant thigh
And sat her on it for a while
As he held forth, in Stoic style:
"Oh, life, old life! Egad!" he cried,
"Almost afore we've lived we've died!
The Bible says: ALL FLESH IS GRASS –
Doubt that 'n you're a silly arse!
Be'n't nothin' permanent, as such –
All things is tarnished by Time's touch –
Just look at me – one moment 'ere,
On top o' things, in mid career
Of pride and pomp – the next, cut down!
Strung up, that is – in old York town!
Ay, 'tis the poxy way o' things –

E'en at the palace gates o' kings
Death knocks! 'Oo said that? I dunnow.
'E knew 'is bloody onions, though!
'E spoke the truth, or I'll be blowed!"
"Horace, that is – Book one, fourth ode,"
Said Algie (from whom knowledge flowed
With a momentum of its own).
"A book-learn'd lad! I might o' known
From them there glasses on yer nose –
Arxfud, or Coimbrudge, Oi suppose…"
"Cambridge. I wouldn't be caught dead
In bloody Oxford," Algie said.
"That so? Well, *Oi'll* learn *this* to *thee*:
You seize yer time, while time there be.
Life's a good dish, and you should try it –
You look as though you're on a diet."

He slurped some wine and then fell quiet
While the wench stroked his tousled hair
And an expression of despair
Darkened his marvellous, murderous face.
"Pish! You know that in any case.
But dead! At thirty-five year old!
And ne'er a chance to spend me gold!
I counts me blessin's, I's no fool,
But all the same, 'tis passin' cruel
To leave the play afore it ends –
'Twere 'ard, 'twere 'arsh, 'twere *Life*, my friends,
Old Life itself! I tells ye what:
Me loot's still out there, like as not,
'Tis on that 'eath, 'n no mistake.
You find it, now, for old Dick's sake,
You find it, and you spend it – live

For *me!*"
She wasn't positive
But mightn't Turpin be the one?
He fairly *fizzled* with *élan.*
"He *is* a ghost, and that might pose
Some problems, but one never knows…"
His IQ didn't seem immense,
Amounting more to common sense
Or cracker-barrel wisdom, but
What did that matter when he cut
So fine a figure? Who'd *not* fall
For one so handsome, well-built, tall?
He stirred her loins in various ways:
His mere demeanour, *mien,* would raise
The coldest woman's temperature –
So confident, yet not cocksure
(His sadness rescued him from that)
And he'd the book of charm off pat –
"So dead," she thought, "yet so alive!"
  They drank, their friend held forth till five,
And then, as rosy-fingered dawn
Began to rustle up the morn
Dick Turpin pulled his pistol out
And fired a shot which took a gout
Out of the ceiling. Hearing it,
Away the ghosts began to flit –
They drained their tankards dry and hit
The spectral road. Away they stole
To God knows where. The watering-hole
Itself did not take off, but changed –
Bits came, bits went, were rearranged
Into the somewhat blander one

Where folk still drink, three centuries on.
  Lucy and Algie crossed the Heath
With Turpin's talk of life and death
And loot still ringing in their ears,
Resolved that, if it took them years,
They'd not betray their new-found friend –
They would track down, dig up, and spend
Dick Turpin's buried treasure.

FIVE

"Fine,"
Said Algie. "We'll be there at nine.
Byee." And he replaced the 'phone.
One Saturday not spent alone –
Even unworldly Algernon
Was mildly pleased, and muttered: "Bon!"
      So, minutes before nine o'clock,
Lucy, in her best party frock,
And Algie, in a crumpled suit
With bits of lining poking through it
To show his life was "of the mind",
Passed Hampstead tube station and climbed
A set of old Dickensian steps
Up which the panting traveller schleps
To get from Heath Street to the Mount -
Forty-four steps at my last count -
With ramps between – it's quite a climb -
I'll deal with it some other time -
Anyway, up it they must wend.
      Algernon had a bosom friend
A buddy from his Oxford days
Named Mungo, who had won high praise
For the chic gallery he ran
Upon a heterogeneous plan -
Deliberately, *perversely* so –
Just that, in fact, made people go -
Old mixing nervously with new –
Pre-Raphaelites and people who
Drowned canvasses, without restraint

Or talent, in mere, pointless paint.

    The steps that I made mention of
A dozen lines or so above
Were those beyond which Mungo had
His chic and well-appointed pad
And, since the factory of fame
Had manufactured him a name,
Art, music, literature – the whole
Quasi-industrial rigmarole
That is the Culture of our time
Was slogging up the Northern Line
To Hampstead, and his smart duplex.
There Mungo would reward their treks
With conversation (clever tosh)
And very decent booze and nosh.

    "Hell-*oooo*, my darlings!" Mungo cried,
How fab to see you! Step inside!
You join me on a day of woe –
A *rock-star's* just moved in below!"
(He spoke the word with a distaste
Suited to someone so misplaced
In this vile world, this age of lead,
This tawdry, tacky, trite… 'nuff said.)
He was as slender as a crane;
As if to cool his red-hot brain
His hair was militarily shorn,
His manner, languid, and forlorn,
His orientation, far from clear –
Probably neither there nor here.
Tonight he wore a white as milk
Kimono of Kyoto silk –
A damned expensive one, at that.

The salient feature of his flat
Was a vast window with a view
Which Lucy went straight over to.
You saw it all from Mungo's home –
Shard, BT Tower, Eye, Gherkin, Dome
Spread out iconically below –
To each of them a floodlight's glow
Imparted emblematic power -
Cool city, city of the hour –
Far off, Canary Wharf, its tower
Whose ever-flashing, lonely light
Sent out its signal through the night
To all the other lights around,
As if it sought, but never found
A mate to come and live with it.
These lights, in turn, were all *moon*-lit,
Nature thereby reminding man
He's just one item in Her plan.

    A bloke, unbidden, brought some wine
In lieu of any chat-up line
And filled a glass, and gave it her -
A painter, whose credentials were,
As he divulged without demur,
A reputation, growing fast
For canvases that could be classed
Not really as *expressionist*
(She wondered if he might be pissed
Or stoned, that he should bang on so
To somebody he didn't know)
Nor as conceptual, nor abstract –
"Nor *anything*, in actual fact.
They're mainly dots and stripes," he said.

"'Course, Matthew Collings wants me dead,
Well, balls to him. I'm making pots.
The Krauts like stripes, the Yanks like dots –
Must be a racial thing, I guess.
Fancy a shag? … Is that a yes?
I sometimes leave the canvas blank."
  Clearly this fellow's paintings stank,
He just sold canvas by the yard.
His Rothko act was a charade.
She always called a spade a spade
And would have gone out on a limb
And told him what she thought of him
But never got the chance, because
He blathered on without a pause
For half an hour, and then they ate.
Lucy was dying to relate
The story of their escapade
With Turpin, but she got waylaid
By quite a tedious writer there
Who'd been translating Molière
And couldn't witter on enough
About "my version of *Tartuffe*".
But she did speak at length – and told
The story of Dick Turpin's gold –
How she and Algie and Turpin
Had hobnobbed at the Spaniards Inn
After they'd met him on the Heath
And how he'd mused on life and death
In maudlin vein. She also spoke
Of how he'd stowed the swag, poor bloke,
Got from the carriages he'd looted,
Then clean forgotten where he'd put it!

Mungo was either disinclined
To think her mad, or didn't mind –
"Well, Lucy! What a story! Wow!
You mean he lost his memory? How?
Don't speak! I *know*! It's quite a tale…
You may have heard of Mrs Thrale?
A friend of Johnson's? No? No matter."
(He sighed, and passed her the cheese platter)
"*Dear* Mrs Thrale – no, she can wait.
Well now, in Seventeen Thirty-Eight,
When Turpin was still on the loose,
With three good years before the noose,
An equally amazing man,
A mad Italian charlatan
And wizard – one "Count" Cagliostro
Had come to London. What a pro!
The king of conmen – scams galore
He pulled, and was notorious for.
He posed as an Italian lord –
In fact he was a thief, a fraud,
No more a count than me or you –
His blood was very far from blue –
Palermo's backstreets gave him birth –
One of the hellholes of God's earth –
It was charisma, brains, and wit
That got Cagliostro out of it.
Thence to St Petersburg and back
As magus, mountebank and quack –
All Europe was his stamping ground,
Oh, brother, did he get around,
Hoodwinking everyone he'd meet,
Making a fortune through deceit –

Where was I? Shit! I've lost the thread…
Ah, yes – this count, who, as I said,
Was just a rogue, with no more blue
Blood in his veins than me or you,
Despite his dubious renown,
Was lodging, while he was in town,
With *Mrs Thrale's* papa. Why *he*
Should put the scoundrel up, search me"
(He passed the vintage port to her)
"But strange liaisons do occur.
Well, in the Mitre Inn one day
Some gamesters had sat down to play
A round or two of *vingt-et-un* –
This Count Cagliostro being one,
Turpin another. Turpin won.
He won for hours without respite –
Something was obviously not right
But no one dared to intervene,
Or challenge Dick, and make a scene –
He was too murderous and mean.
Well, Turpin told them, while they played,
How, from each coach that he waylaid,
He kept some loot back – as he said
'Against a rainy day 'n that.'
(If so, then we were looking at
A very rainy day indeed)
'Ye never knows when ye moight need
A little extra set aside,'
So he observed with quiet pride,
'Oi've got moi nestegg safely stored,
Indeed, 'tis quite a decent 'oard,
Some of it's *buried*, in a chest…'

At cards, if Turpin came of *best*
The one whose purse was really *hurt*
Was Cagliostro, who lost his shirt,
Every last sovereign he possessed
Wound up in Turpin's treasure chest.
He quickly got his own back, though –
And here's the part you'll want to know –
They met for cards a second time
And when they did, he drugged Dick's wine –
A drug that made his memory fail
Though Dick blamed too much wine, or ale.
Cagliostro had one end in view:
To make sure Dick no longer knew
Where he had stashed his scads of loot –
The sly count didn't care a hoot
About the money, no, not he –
His goal was reciprocity.
He got it: the drug did the trick
And from thenceforward poor old Dick
Could not think *where* he'd put his hoard."

     She thought this story might afford
Great-Aunt Alicia some fun
(Since she'd complained of having none)
So Lucy told it her next day.
"Cagliostro? Oh! My sweet conte!
What halcyon days those were! Ah, yes!"
The witch cried, and a tear, no less –
A human fragment, so to speak -
Coursed down her supernatural cheek
Mio caro conte! What a chap!
Well, they were practically on tap
In those days, were amazing men,

But *he* was special, even then –
A living legend, yes indeed! –
Leastways, before he went to seed
And wound up in an Iti jail.
Cagliostro! Thereby hangs a tale!
Ah, yes, such men! Where are they now?"
"Then you were friends?" – "My dear, and how!
He was a *wizard*, – or, that is,
It was a favourite *claim* of his –
But one I always felt was rash,
And if we ever were to clash,
If I may make so bold to say,
My magic would blow *his* away."
"And were you… ?" – "Yes – for a short time.
Far too addicted, though, to crime,
But lacked the skill to make it pay –
Cooked up some new scam every day –
The *Diamond Necklace* – sad affair –
The nitwit really slipped up there –
He was a mason too, you know -
Oh, dear me, yes! Count Cagliostro!"
(Her green eyes fairly misted over
As she recalled her former lover.)
"My, my, what memories you've brought back.
He *was* a wizard in the sack!
It might make sense to quiz him – eh?
And find out what he has to say
About Dick Turpin. What d'you think?
That drug he dropped into his drink –
Suppose there were an antidote?
Get some of that down Turpin's throat,
It brings him back his memory,

And bang! Hey presto! You're home free!
Venice is quite a place. Been there?
Yeees! I could use a change of air –
It's such a captivating spot –
Cagliostro lives there – tell you what:
We'll go and see him. What d'you say?"
"In Venice! When?" – "Why not today?
Why even wait to catch our breath?
On this point I am with Macbeth."
" 'If 'twere done when 'twere done' you mean?"
"That's right. Act One. Forget which scene.
My sister Sibyl's also there –
She's living just off Saint Mark's Square –
She'll put us up. Let's not delay.
Fetch Algie, and we're on our way."

SIX

Few things can beat a broomstick ride
Over the English countryside.
'Twixt London and the Kentish coast
The landscape can have kept, at most,
Half of the beauty it once had
But even so it's not half bad
With rolling hills and verdant fields
And forests (few can match the Weald's)
A village green, an ancient church -
Features that make the stomach lurch
In a strange, half nostalgic way,
As if the past still lived today –
A pastoral idyll, what remains
To make it perfect, but the strains
Of Elgar playing in the mind,
Purcell, Vaughan-Williams – any kind
Of music made for plunging one
Into a dream of Albion…
A little Georgian market town –
A hedgerow that's not been cut down –
A sunlit meadow that still might
Be decked in yellow or in white
By cow-parsley or buttercup –
Oh, England, England! Oh, shut up!
        They skirted France, I can't think why,
You'd cross it as the crow would fly
But Aunt Alicia veered off East.
Despite the load their speed increased –
Fast as a flash of lightning, greased,

They whizzed past Germany, but then,
Above the Alps, slowed down again
So Lucy got a proper look.
That was the route Alicia took.
Brooms run on supernatural power:
They'd not been in the air an hour
When they glimpsed, glinting in the sun,
Second in loveliness to none,
Part brilliant azure, part ablaze
Where it had caught the high sun's rays,
A sheet of psychedelic blue
Suddenly swinging into view –
Lucy's first sight of that great sea
That cinctures most of Italy.
"There are a lot more fish in that
Or I shall eat my pointed hat!"
The witch said, with a filthy grin
At Lucy. They were coming in,
At fast reducing speed, to land,
And they could see, on their right hand,
Standing as sentry to the bay,
Santa Maria Salute,
And then another strip of blue –
The Grand Canal, that great Who's Who
Of Western culture – Verdi there,
Here Wagner, Byron – everywhere
Some genius or other's pad,
Such great inhabitants it's had –
Proust, Goethe, Titian, and the rest -
One sees, and almost feels oppressed –
Could wish their palaces would sink
Into the sea, whose waters stink.

At one end of a square, Saint Marks'
Strange architectural hybrid parks
Its stately bulk. And who would think
Of painting his whole house bright pink?
Yet that is what the Doge has done –
By golly it's a gorgeous one
But pinker than a flamingo,
Which some may find a tad de trop.
      Oh, Venice, Venice! What a place!
For all they've vanished without trace,
Forever lost in history's haze,
Those glorious, those halcyon days,
When Moneteverdi penned *Ulisse*
And if you merely blinked you'd miss a –
Oh, I don't know, a Titian nude,
So sensual, without being rude,
Or something of Carpaccio's,
Or Byron's verse, or Ruskin's prose,
And Casanova, in a gondola,
Would woo a girl, and stroke and fondle her -
How painfully I feel their lack –
That's why I've taken Lucy back
Two centuries, or a little more,
In fact, to Seventeen Ninety-Four.
      A witch can change her shape or hue
While powerful ones, if minded to,
Can travel back through centuries
To any point in time they please.
Great-Aunt Alicia could perform
That feat: for her it was the norm,
To flit off to some other age
When *this* one put her in a rage

Or bored her, as it often did.
Thus, now, they landed, not amid
A swarm of tourists snapping shots
Of five or six compulsory spots,
Not in the *touristique mêlée*
That is the Venice of today –
A two-day-stop-offy, postcardy
Nightmare, but in the city Guardi
And Canaletto used to paint –
So gorgeous it could make you faint.
    Aunt Sibyl's palace stood upon
A small canal, a smelly one,
Smellier even than the Grand,
And there it was they came to land,
On an old, rotting quay. A *calle*
(Venetian for a narrow alley)
That reeked of putridness and must
Hugged the decrepit yet august
Palazzo on its southern side.
This *calle* being three feet wide
They walked in single file, and then
Emerged into the light again
To find a little, ancient, low
Seventeenth century portico
And oak door, at which Lucy knocked
And which a butler soon unlocked.
He eyed them with myopic squint,
Then all at once a gleeful glint
Lit his glaucomatous old eyes
As he appeared to recognise
Great-Aunt Alicia: *"No! Sei tu?"*
He cried (which means: "No! Is it you?")

She didn't flinch at being *tu*'d
Though actually it was quite rude
And *lei* was what he should have said.
But climbed the four stone steps which led
Up to the door, then stepped inside.
There Great-Aunt Sibyl stood, moist-eyed
To see, after so many years,
Her cherished sister. Many tears,
Indeed, were shed by both old crones
Before, in trembling, joyous tones,
They exchanged greetings, whooped, and hugged,
While off the ancient porter lugged
The trunk the travellers had brought
And Lucy wondered if he ought
Since plainly he lacked strength enough,
So loudly did he huff and puff,
And was in evident distress.
     Aunt Sibyl wasn't slow to guess
Just what had brought her sister here:
"You want to see him, don't you dear?
Oh, don't get all abashed and coy –
You want to see your old toy-boy,
Cagliostro. Well, we'll have him round
Assuming that he's to be found –
I'll send a servant to his place –
Don't worry, dear, I'm on the case –
He'll come to dine – this evening, even –
Splendid! A party! We'll be seven –
That's right, I have another guest –
A *nabob*, let it be confessed,
And not just *any* nabob – no,
This one's a *Sanskrit scholar!*"

So

A servant called on Cagliostro,
Asked could he come, he promised to,
And bring "a friend" (he'd not say who).
The cook went well-nigh through the roof
At such short notice, yet gave proof
Of matchless culinary skill,
And, as the sun's rays touched the sill
And ceased their long day's dazzling,
The party was in full, fine swing.

Do we not all, at moments, yearn
For youth's insouciance to return?
Wish that we might, for one day, be
Forty pounds lighter, and carefree,
Reverse Time's ever-rolling tide,
As Botox, and the like, have tried,
And singularly failed, to do?
Hats off, then, to the witches, who,
Though they were, even at that date,
One seven centuries old, one eight,
Now shed the marring marks of Time
And came down looking quite sublime,
Two angels, but with diamond rings
And pearls for haloes and for wings,
Clad, in the fashion of the age,
In dresses whose décolletage
With its outrageous, reckless plunge,
Invited the seducer's lunge.
Lucy had dressed in the same style -
For beauty she was off the dial –
A living Gainsborough, or Boucher
(The latter's best is Miss O'Shea -

She's posed in such a fetching way
With her... her... no, I'd best not say)
She quite eclipsed her two great-aunts –
Cleopatra would have stood no chance.
  Cagliostro'd said he'd bring a chum –
Who should it be with whom he'd come?
Only the chief erotic toast
Of all of Europe, history's most
Illustrious, industrious lover,
Si'or Giacomo di Casanova!
His chief impact consisted in
The contrast of his tawny skin
And snow-white wig. Cagliostro's eyes
Were *his* great strength: he'd mesmerise
A person with his manic stare
As might a headlight do a hare.
The nabob saw him and said: "Lawd!
'Tis he! The gweat Italian fwaud!
Egad!" And "Count" Cagliostro glared.
  A sucking pig had been prepared
And a tremendous smell of meat
Regaled them as they sat to eat –
A fine aroma which, to me,
Is twice as sweet as *Givenchy*.
The nabob, well aware that it's
The privilege of high-class Brits
To dominate things totally
Wherever they may chance to be,
Began to speak, or rather, bray,
With many a "Demmit!" and "I say!"
And without anyone's inviting
About a book that he was writing –

Translating – straight from the Sanskrit -
Horseplay – that was the gist of it –
A treatise on the Art of Love:
When to be under, when above,
Or, for the very fit and keen,
When to be somewhere in between.
"There's a position in it, Sir…
But, ladies pwesent, I demur…"
"Oh, don't demur for *us*, my dear,"
Alicia cried, "we *long* to hear."
"It's called *The Scorpion With Two Backs*,"
Said he, "and I believe 'twould tax
The ablest lover; I've long thought it
Impossible, 'tis so contorted."
"Impossible? Diavolo!"
Cried Casanova. "*You* say so!
I'll do it!" (He was in a rage.)
"I'll do it now! Show me the page!"
The nabob said he'd have it brought,
They'd scrutinize it over port.

      The vintages of Veneto
Had flowed now for three hours or so
Alicia was sat beside
Cagliostro, whom she slyly plied
With wine – filled and refilled his glass -
Most would have gone tit over arse
If they had drunk as much as that
But not Cagliostro – there he sat
Bibbing continuously, and burpin'
But sober.
When she mentioned Turpin,
Hoping to ambush him and worm

Out of him what she wished to learn,
She found him quick, evasive, shrewd
And clearly not the least bit stewed.
Immediately he smelled a rat
And said: "Eh? Why you speak of dat?"
"No reason." "Eh? You shoot some line?"
"Not in the least... You... drugged his wine...
They say you drugged it... Is it true?"
"What if it be? Woss dat to you?"
"Oh... nothing..." "You ged uppa my nose."
"Sorry to hear it... I suppose
There'd be an antidote...? You see
The subject really interests me –
I'm mad on pharmacology."
"You try de patience of de saint!
Per'aps there his, per'aps there hain't."
From this Alicia guessed there was –
She didn't press him, though, because
He had begun to scowl and pout –
Anyway, she'd found *something* out.

　　After the ladies had withdrawn
The nabob said: "The gels have gawn
We'll have that book bwought, don't ye know –
It will astonish you." And so
A servant fetched it. The nabob
Had done a really first-rate job:
Not only had the text been put
Into the choicest English, but,
Being a gifted artist, too,
He'd illustrated it right through
By copying the original plates.
The two Italians mopped their pates –

This steamy volume made them sweat
For how salacious could you get?
The pictures of cavorting lovers
Writhing about between its covers
Made Aretino's work look tame.
Sex seemed a pretty complex game
When played the Ancient Indian way -
That's if one had the nerve to play.
Now, Casanova, leafing through
And finding Number Sixty-Two,
The *Scorpion With Two Backs*, maintained
That, though some muscles might get strained,
It could be done, and he would try –
"For H-onour, and for H-italy."

    In the *salotto*, later on,
After the custom, everyone
Was back together, taking tea
When Lucy, happening to see
An instrument, exclaimed: "Good Lord!
Aunt Sibyl has a harpsichord!"
"Yes, *not a virginals!*" said she,
Chuckling, and winking wickedly
At Aunt Alicia, "do you play?"
"A little." – "Splendid! Fire away!"

    So Lucy sat down and began.
She started with some Couperin,
Playing with careless, brilliant ease,
Her fingers flew across the keys,
What virtuosity, what… flair!
She dazzled everyone there,
First with the Couperin, then Scarlatti.
Music, you mollify the ratty,

Breed sweetness in the nasty creep,
Soothe the insomniac to sleep,
Relax the tense, endow the weak
With strength – and make the sexless geek,
Who never yet has been on fire,
Suddenly flare up with desire…
As now you did to Algernon.
For, as his cousin rattled on,
A yearning formed in him – a sense
Of something stronger, more intense
Than he had ever felt before:
Amor, amore, love, amour,
Call it whatever name you will
There is no void it cannot fill
And it was filling his up now
Although he had no notion how
A woman should be won or wooed -
His learning didn't quite include
That subject, so he sat there, mute,
And might as well have been a newt
For all the fat deflowering use he
Could possibly have been to Lucy.

    Algie was not the only one
She'd made a strong impression on -
No, Casanova's ear, and eye
Were equally enchanted by
Lucy's performance. "Che diletto!"
He murmured, "Che dolce pezzetto!"
She'd all but turned his ruthless head
And he would have her in his bed
Before the stars had quit the sky
Or want to know the reason why.

SEVEN

She'd lit the great man's fire, all right.
He found her a complete delight.
Lucy, aware she'd caught his eye,
Was kissing chastity goodbye,
In thought, at any rate. Tonight
Would see the end of her sad plight...
"Tonight my cherry shall be plucked...
At last, I'm going to be... Fine!"
She thought, "and talk about high time!
He'll know his stuff – he's Casanova,
He's *famed* for it the whole world over.
He talks well. All Italians do –
No men know better how to woo
If racial stereotypes are true.
So it's all bullshit. Should I care?
I've *got* to get deflowered, so there!
(She told herself) "We're on! Hooray!
He fits the bill – it's bombs away!"
        Her thoughts ran on in this lewd groove
But Casanova made no move.
Could all his ogling have meant
Nothing at all? Away he went,
That great Rococo superman,
Having done nothing bolder than
To bow the once and kiss her hand.
Why? Lucy couldn't understand.
When he'd been watching her all night
As might a mongoose watch a krait!
        That night she couldn't sleep, though weary,

"Jesus," she thought, "but life is dreary!
The awful ravelled sleeve of care –
Shakespeare refers to it somewhere –
Sleep's meant to knit it up, he says,
Care's ravelled *my* poor sleeve – oh, yes!
Ravelled it past all knitting up!
I've yet again been sold a pup!
I mean, it looked to be a *must* –
His eyes were *sparkling* with lust!
Then Algie didn't turn a hair
When I accosted him, half bare,
And Richard turned into a hare...
Men! Messing with our heads for sport!
Or am I less cute than I thought?
Yes, I'm afraid it must be that."

    Meanwhile, downstairs, Alicia sat
With Count Cagliostro, and some port.
"Fancy a card-game of some sort?"
She said. "I brought a pack with me..."
"Carte? Ma, per che no?" said he,
(Translation: "Cards? We could do worse.")
The witch brought out a bulging purse,
He gaped and goggled when he saw it –
"The antidote – I'll play you for it:
I lose, you get this purse; I win,
You tell me how to cure Turpin."
"Madonna! Dat dere purse must hold
More dan-a fifty pound in gold!
Ees habsolutely what I need!"
The count thought, slavering with greed.
"A single hand of *vingt-et-un?"*
Alicia said. *"Va bene! Done!"*

She dealt the bogus count a ten,
Herself a seven, which she then,
Turned, by a quickly muttered spell,
Metamorphosed it as it fell,
Into a ten. Cagliostro's luck
Was in. A second ten. He stuck.
Now he was shouting: "See? I won!
Venti! Stupendo!" *"Vingt-et-un,"*
The witch said, and revealed an ace,
Her second card. Cagliostro's face
Went whiter, when he saw that card,
Than snow, or chalk, or milk, or lard.
He could have killed her then and there –
"You use de magic! Ees no fair!"
He shrieked. "I could 'ave done de same
But I no cheat – I play de game."
"What piffle! Done the same, indeed!
Like Hell, you boastful, bogus weed!
That spell was way beyond your scope.
You know you never had a hope."
"You cheat! I geeve no hantidote!
That Turpin guy – he get-a my goat!
I no release him from de drug!
De crazy, murdering, Heengleesh thug!"
What-a you do? You cheat me, eh?
You Breeteesh meant to love fair play!"
"Oh, have the damned purse anyway,"
Alicia said, "if it'll stop
Your gibbering, you whining wop!
Now, what's the antidote? Tell me."
"Ees simple – jus' an 'erbal tea
Wid sage and thyme and meadow grass –

One cup, and de hamnesia pass."
    The voice of a young gondolier
Who'd tied his vessel to the pier
And had begun to sing a long,
Romantic, sad, Venetian song
Drifted across from the lagoon
And floated into Lucy's room
Whose windows were all open wide.
She heard the yearning strains, and sighed –
The lyric, she imagined, told
Of some Venetian lass of old
Whose trouble, if not quite the same
As hers, had still brought grief and shame,
And her emotions had but one vent:
A canal's bottom, or a convent
(That's two vents, but because I'm loath
To lose the rhyme, I'll keep them both)
Their plights, then, were the same, except
That she had lost what Lucy'd kept.

    Then, through the open casement, leapt
The man himself – he'd changed his mind!
(Or so she modestly opined –
In fact he'd had but one idea –
Just waited till the coast was clear.)
Lucy's deflated self-esteem
Got up a sudden head of steam -
Such turnabouts do bolster you
And make one bonk as good as two.
Having bestowed this ego-boost
Her lover, from his coat, produced
Two pages of the nabob's book –
The first (at which she blushed to look)

Depicted two young lovers, in
Some weird extremity of sin
And intertwined like lengths of flax.
"Is that *The Scorpion With Two Backs* –
The one the nabob said must be
Impossible?" asked Lucy. *"Si!"*
She scanned the picture, much perplexed
(The other page contained the text)
The pictured pair'd pursued their pleasure
Beyond all due and proper measure,
Were inextricably entwined,
Their bodies seemed to have combined
In almost an *arachnoid* way
But Lucy stifled her dismay,
She wasn't easy to deter,
She'd do this if it crippled her,
Her cherry must, and would, be lost
No matter what the losing cost.
        They were attempting quite a feat,
For intricacy, hard to beat,
More tortuous sex seldom got –
In fact, a literal love-knot.
"Take off your nightdress, if you please
And I shall just get rid of these,"
 Commanded the old randy goat
And doffed his breeches and his coat.
So now they stood there, both stark nude.
"I must adopt this attitude...
My left leg under yours... *così*...
Now stretch right out and straddle me...
And take my hand... and pull, *cosà*...
Sinistra... *left* hand... *eccola*!

Now, *spingi*! Push! With all your might!
Your *gamba destra* here – your right!
****

Oof! *Eccellente!* Can you sit?
Good! Here we go – the hardest bit –
I lift my rear, you lower yours…
Me upside down, you on all fours…
Now I just twist around like so…
Now you… Good girl! *Bravissimo!*
Except that you're a bit too low…
Up! Up, Lucia! *Alzati!*
Ohimé! We're not how we should be!
You must bestride me still, but not…
Dio! We've gone awry! Now what?
We should be in a firm embrace -
One leg's not in its proper place –
But which one? *Zitto! Mama mia!*
We're locked together! Dear oh dear!"

And locked they were – as tight as glue.
"What are we going to damned well do?"
Screamed Lucy, who had had enough.
"I thought you knew your ****ing stuff!"

How frightful to be stuck so fast –
Two pieces of elastoplast,
Two mayflies at the height of May
Could not be closer joined than they,
He with his **** just hanging free,
Dangling down redundantly,
She with her bottom in the air,
Limbs here, and there, and everywhere,
You couldn't tell, as they now were,
Which bits were him and which were her.

They shouted: "Help!" No time for shame,
And, in a dubious form, help came:
The nabob and the two great-aunts.
"Didn't I tell 'im? Not a chance,"
Triumphantly exclaimed the Brit,
"Or else I mistwanslated it!"
The great-aunts caterwauled with glee
At such obscene absurdity
But Lucy then began to yell:
"Just separate us! Use a spell!"
"No earthly magic that I know
 Can sort out *this* imbroglio!"
Said Aunt Alicia. "Sibyl, dear,
Can you apply *your* knowledge here?
Have you a quacksalve for the nonce?"
"I knew a handsome raja once,
Or rather, not exactly *knew*,
This being in Eighteen-Sixty-Two -
I'm *going* to know him. You're in luck:
We'll try the *Scorpion*, and get stuck,
During a durbar in Calcutta –
What rescues us is *heaps of butter.*"
    As a solution it was neat:
The butter – twelve pats – worked a treat,
A plain but versatile resource.
Lucy, although relieved, of course,
Awoke next morning quite distraught
That ill luck had contrived to thwart
Her quest once more. On gruesome form
She was – within her raged a storm
Though outside the Italian sun
Already blazed, and had begun,

By ten, to animate the stones
Of Venice, heightening their tones
And proving Monet got it right
About old buildings and sunlight.
     After some misty-eyed goodbyes
Again they journeyed through the skies
And Lucy was allowed to see some
More parts of Europe from the besom.
Her great-aunt gurgled in her throat
With glee: "I got the antidote!"
She whooped. "It's all here, in my noddle.
To cure Dick ought to be a doddle."
A kindly twinkle lit her eye
As on they hurtled through the sky.
So *something* had been salvaged, then,
From a disastrous trip.
But when,
After an hour or so, they neared
Hampstead, and far below appeared
Saint John's churchyard, each slab, each tomb
Plunged Lucy deeper into gloom.
It concentrates the mind, alright,
A sombre and a chilling sight
It is, that great, macabre fleet,
At anchor just above Heath Street,
Of vessels in their final port –
Theirs, everybody's last resort.
"Ah, death!" the witch said, "Where's thy sting?
And yet you lurk in everything.
Know what I think the secret is?
Of life, I mean… don't laugh at this,
It's a cliché, but one that works,

In which a grain of real truth lurks -
It's knowing what you *want*, my dear –
Keeping your wishes *sharp* and clear,
Be they a yearning, or a cause,
I'm not so sure you've *sorted* yours.
What is it, child, for which you wish?
Why can't you simply land a fish?
Few nets have been more *feebly* cast!
I have to tell you, I'm aghast
At your ineptitude thus far –
Each chance you get you promptly mar!"
"We're talking about two, to date,"
Said Lucy, just a tad irate,
"And it was *you yourself* that wrecked
The first one, as I recollect!"
"Don't say there weren't a few before?"
"Yes, and there's doubtless loads in store –
I'm certain it'll happen soon –
Christ, I'm not asking for the moon!"
Came Lucy's quick and sharp riposte,
"My wretched cherry will be lost
Before another year is out,
Of that I won't admit a doubt!"
"That's if you really *want* a mate,"
Alicia said. "Your conscious state
May seem to, but I can't avoid
A nod to dear old Dr Freud;
I knew him, and I dare avow
That he'd have sussed you out by now
As someone whose unconscious aim
And conscious wish are not the same.
I don't know why I mention it,

Save that the fickle moments flit,
At speed, and even as I speak,
Past you, and maybe by next week -
There being no reckoning with Fate
Which sometimes seems prepared to wait,
Sometimes (and this is why I worry)
To be in an infernal hurry –
You too, dear, will be one of those
Enjoying (or not) their last repose."
She pointed grimly down, with this,
At Hampstead's old necropolis.
"I have a wish, I know I do,
There *is* a quarry I pursue,
It's just elusive," Lucy mused,
"And surely I can be excused
For having failed to catch it yet:
There's been a hindrance or a let
At every turn!"
Though she was young
Her aunt had put a cat among
Her mental pigeons, so to speak –
Time waits for no man. Feeling bleak
She looked back at the graves below,
Row upon disconcerting row,
" 'Gather ye rosebuds while ye may.'
'Eheu, fugaces, Postume...'[*]
Life is first boredom and then fear
Then it evaporates – oh dear!"
Sighed Lucy, all but overcome
With thoughts both literate and glum.

---

[*]Alas, Postumus, the fleeting (years slip away) – *Horace Odes* II xiv

But Algie was oblivious to
The sight of Death's eternal crew –
The boy was horribly in love,
Anything else he wot not of,
But suffered, tortured, torn apart.
Racked with a swelling, aching heart
He couldn't speak, but merely moon,
Perched on the back end of the broom.
    The magic mansion was in sight,
A one-man architectural blight,
Its daft adornments all on view –
Pinnacle, turret, curlicue,
All shining in the morning sun,
Such an abode as might have done,
Nay, would have been the ideal spot
Say, for the Lady of Shallot,
Or else King Arthur, when in town,
An urban Camelot, scaled down,
For sunlight did the place no harm,
Gave it a sort of *anti-charm*,
A certain something, almost style,
An aspect not *entirely vile*,
This poor old house I've pilloried.
They neared it at reducing speed
Till an unceremonious dip
Ended their supernatural trip.
"Ah! Home!" the witch was moved to cry
And brushed a tear from one green eye.
"Ah! Home!" But that was all. They dived
As I just said, and thus arrived
Once more upon the rabbit-gnawn,
Weedy but well-beloved front lawn.

EIGHT

They had a single end in view –
Well, Lucy, obviously, had two
But this had now become a quest
That she pursued with equal zest:
To give the antidote to Dick
And preferably double quick.
The trouble was, he'd disappeared
Skedaddled, scarpered, vanished – weird!
They tried the Spaniards every night
But it was empty. At first light
They'd grab a few hours' sleep, and then
Go straight back to the Heath again,
And dig, not knowing where to start,
Just trying any random part.
And while they wondered where he'd slunk
The antidote remained undrunk.
Till that herb tea had set in train
The healing process in Dick's brain,
Had coursed restoratively through it,
He'd not know where he'd stashed his loot,
The outlook was becoming grim,
Weeks passed, and still no sign of him.
    Algernon's love for Lucy grew,
They took a harmless stroll or two,
Had tea at Kenwood, unaware
That, all the while, a jealous hare
Was watching, waiting for a chance
To thwart their blossoming romance.
Each morning he'd pick up their scent

And tail them everywhere they went.
But Algernon made Lucy wait –
He'd dither and prevaricate,
Until the girl began to doubt
Whether he'd ever ask her out.
It was frustrating! Ever since
The Venice trip, she'd dropped broad hints
But still he wouldn't take the bait.
"We'll never get there at this rate,
I'll have to take the lead," she thought,
"The desperate woman's last resort -
I'll have to make some kind of lunge."
    But then, at last, he took the plunge.
He didn't do it with much grace –
"I…wondered… if you knew a place
Where we might go and eat," said he,
"*I* shall be paying – probably."
She smiled. "I'm happy to go Dutch,"
She told him, "if it costs too much."
"No, no, I'll pay. Where shall we go?
Hogwoods in Heath Street's, well, so so…
I work till seven. Let's say… eight?"
"Cool."
Jesus, was he in a state!
He'd barely reached his room before
He let out a triumphant roar,
Put some Ravel on *(Couperin's Tomb)*
And started dancing round the room,
Doing great leaps and pirouettes,
As bad as human folly gets
It was. Alicia saw the boy
Suddenly full of mindless joy,

His mammoth intellect awry,
And wasn't slow to fathom why.
"The idiot's in love, of course,
As bad as Romeo, or worse,
He's acting like a bloody fool.
Pity – till now he seemed quite cool."
While ruminating in this wise
She did find time to sympathize:
"It's very silly, that's for sure,
The boy's extremely immature,
Emotionally, anyway,
But that defect cannot outweigh
His simply *staggering* IQ –
I should forgive him, and I do –
He is my grandson, after all."

Like some young deb before a ball,
While time dragged by and romance beckoned
Algie was counting every second.
The waiting made him fuss and fret -
He took *huge* care with his toilette -
Though mainly out of vanity
It also helped the time go by.
He bathed, then bathed again for luck,
And this although he had no truck
With hygiene as a general rule –
The province of the idle fool
He deemed it, something far beneath
A *thinker* like himself. His teeth
He brushed for fully half an hour;
Went to his grandmother's boudoir
And splashed himself with all her scents
Until his fragrance was intense;

Her aromatic oils he took
And rubbed them into every nook;
Mascara, powder, were applied;
Hairs plucked, nails filed, skin scarified;
In every mirror that he passed
He checked himself; not least, though last,
His two *suits* drove him round the bend –
Which one to wear? For hours on end
He mulled it over, *and* his shoes,
And shirts – he simply couldn't choose.

    At seven thirty he was dressed
At last, and felt he looked his best,
Or least grotesque, at any rate.
He reached the restaurant at eight.
Lucy was coming separately -
She'd been out buying clothes since three -
Of her, as yet, there was no sign.
How silly to be bang on time -
Waiting, on dates, is such a trial,
Anxiety increasing, while
Time's passage, which has been so slow
All day, accelerates, and now
The minutes fairly *hurtle* by:
He, she, is late – we're wondering why –
We find some explanation which
Will briefly calm our nerves, then switch
Next moment into abject woe,
Keep oscillating to and fro,
It's possibly love's sternest test...
"Oh, Christ!" thought Algie, "I'm depressed!
So much for my romantic dream,
I was the cat that got the cream,

I thought, and now I'm in despair!"
Then he looked up, and standing there
Was Lucy, looking like a queen.
"A suicide at Golders Green -
Held up for half an hour," she said.
She had on something short, and red
That clung enticingly to her -
He barely saw it through a blur
Of manically delirious bliss –
"Not another comfort like to this,
Succeeds in unknown fate" (Othello
II i) – he'd got it bad, poor fellow!
All heads were turning now, to clock
This babe, and register their shock
That she, who might have oligarchs
Or lords, with money, mansions, parks,
Even perhaps a prince, preferred
A funny-looking little nerd.

     Reader, I've sold you short somewhat,
You surely can't have failed to spot
That nowhere have I yet put in
A *picture* of my heroine –
Touched on her... *outward attributes* –
But each time there's a place that suits
My pc scruples hold me back
"These days you just can't take that tack!"
Says a prim voice inside my head
And I resume my tale instead.
I mentioned that her hair was brown,
A reddish shade, and hung right down
To hide her shoulders. Did I add
(You'd have remembered if I had)

That her… her le… her br… her… Drat!
Can't do it. I *can* tell you that
She was (this gives you some idea)
The kind of beauty who'll appear
While you are visiting a chum
Who's "good with women". Down she'll come,
Descend the lucky bastard's stairs
And catch you wholly unawares
With her astounding pulchritude.
She will be wearing something rude,
Either a skimpy negligée
Or, to your even *worse* dismay,
A *shirt* she's borrowed from your mate;
You'll sit there, mute, and contemplate
Her face, and fabulous contours,
So near, yet never to be yours,
And a great stab of envious pain
Will pierce you, somewhere in your brain
Where memories of failed chat-ups lurk
And sundry dates that didn't work
With girls like her.
"I'm famished! Now,
What have we got here? Snail pilau?
Confit of toad with lemon grass?
Grilled mice? This menu is a farce!"
They ordered, though, and ate, and he
Performed, throughout, imperiously,
Expounding, with supreme aplomb,
The whole of Western Culture, from
The Ancient Greeks to now, and back,
And scattering epigrams like flak.
"My God! He's *thunderously* bright!

Mind-bogglingly erudite!"
Thought Lucy. "Me – I've read a bit –
I'm smart – but I'm a rank half-wit
Compared with him! It *has* to be!
He's *gagging* for it… isn't he?
It's third time lucky, Luce, for you,
And long – no, ages – overdue!"
        I don't know if it was the wine
Or that she'd waited quite some time,
As you've already heard me say,
To get a man and wash away
The taint of chastity, but she
Now leaned across, unflinchingly
And placed a light kiss on his brow,
Was not content with that, and now
Had kissed his lips, which left the geek
Too overcome with joy to speak,
Not on cloud nine, but cloud *nineteen*.
"I know now what the poets mean!
The great love poets of the past!"
He thought, "I've got their point at last!"
(Her foot was touching his.) "This beats
Anything! Sappho, Petrarch, Keats,
Catullus, Dante, Byron, Donne,
I've got them! Grasped them! All in one!
'Tomorrow he that never loved…'*
This is amazing! I've been shoved
Into the Cupid show, head first,

---

*Algie is alluding to the *Pervigilium Veneris*. Cras amet qui
numquam amavit. Quique amavit cras amet. Tomorrow, he who
has never been in love – let him be in love, and let him who has
been in love still be in love.

Without a prompter, unrehearsed!
Don't think about it, or you'll crack!"
"Ay! Keep yer cool and mind yer back,"
Don't flinch, me boy," an echo said –
The voice of Turpin in his head.
"A drop o' rum, per'aps, to soothe
Them nerves, and it'll go as smooth,
Egad it will, as if it were
Old Dick 'imself a-pleasurin' 'er!
Don't fret. There ben't no rule of thumb."
    He downed a Scotch (they had no rum)
And then another one for luck
And then a third ("Oh, what the fuck?")
Then paid the bill. They sauntered down
Flask Walk, in which a fine, full-blown
And unadulterated spring
Was percolating everything
With all the fragrance and immense
Fecundity of its sweet scents,
Pure air, and gently falling dew
As, ambling blissfully, these two,
Oblivious to the period charm
Around them, walked on, arm in arm,
She in her red dress, he on wings –
"This is a spring to end all springs!"
Thought Algie, with a brimming heart,
"Nature's the business! Who needs Art?"
    There were some people still about
Who gawped at them, and found, no doubt,
Sufficient cause to stand and stare
At such a heterogeneous pair.
So ill-matched as to looks, at least –

The boy a visual anti-feast,
The girl astonishing, divine,
A ten, if Venus was a nine.
So frankly fascinated eyes
Followed them, failing to disguise
Amazement at the nymph, who strode
Thus, unabashedly, down the road
With Quasimodo on her arm.
It did his vanity no harm
To read the look on each male face:
"Shit! Why can't *I* be in his place?"
Quite soon the mansion came in sight,
Phantasmal in the velvet night,
Its gargoyles ghostly in the gloom,
Its lancets glinting in the moon.
        They rush upstairs. She puts on jazz.
"What an amazing *shape* she has!"
She strokes his bottom, he strokes hers,
His much-neglected member stirs,
As lust mounts up he starts to sweat,
Clocks her curvaceous silhouette
Against the mullioned window pane;
The thought keeps pounding in his brain:
"This can't be true! This isn't real!"
But true it is, as true as steel.
Her hand is fumbling with his flies,
She stands, a sight to stun all eyes,
Stark nude before him, the red dress
Around her feet. "You've condoms?" "Yes."
(Lord, what a time he'd had in Boots)
"Let's try some sex, then, if that suits!"
He'd started, fumblingly, to grope –

Foreplay? From Algie? Not a hope!
"Just get the condoms." Off he flies
To fetch them, lest his juices rise
(Which would be most inopportune)
Or rather, *overflow*, too soon
(With hormones bottled up for years
Such moments often end in tears)
But, looking in his bedside drawer,
He finds they're not there anymore!

 Was El Dorado ever sought
As desperately as this distraught
Young man now hunted for his Mates?
Was it the cleaner, or the Fates?
Whichever, they were just not there –
Tescos was closed – in blank despair
He shuffled back to Lucy's room
And there the pair sat, plunged in gloom,
Like two frustrated wooden blocks.

 What *had* become of Algie's box
Of condoms? *Fate* was not to blame,
Nor the capricious old beldame,
Before you point your finger at
Alicia; no, the truth is that
They'd found their way to Hampstead Heath –
A *hare* now had them in its teeth.
"I queered that little weirdo's pitch!
And Lucy's, too, the faithless bitch,"
Thought Richard, chuckling in his drey.

 Lucy declared that, come what may,
They mustn't let one fucked-up night
Deter them. "It'll be alright.
We haven't all that long to wait

With Tescos opening at eight
And Boots at… "When's Boots open?" "Nine."
"Relax, then. It'll all be fine."
This lightened Algie's heart of lead
And they went, separately, to bed,
While the great quest for Turpin's gold
Was temporarily placed on hold.

*

"Darn it!" said Turpin, "Missed the brute!
I thought I'd put a ball clean through't!"
Evening was drawing on apace.
(It was the following day, in case
That asterisk and extra space
Have left the matter in the air.)
"Brute" seemed a harsh word for a hare.
It skulked off, hobbling a bit,
For, though not killed, it had been hit
In its hind leg.
He pitied it.
"You would er made a lovely stew!
Well, off you 'op! Away wi' you!
I ain't the 'eart to murder ye
In cold blood, like them swines did me.
Be off, to sorrer, like as not,
'N I'll go 'ome to an empty pot."
Turpin, of course, was prone to gloom.
On certain days it left no room
For other feelings. Then his mood
Would be unbrokenly imbued
With "affect" shrinks call "negative"
"'Tis 'ard bein' dead when ye longs to live,"
He'd mutter, as the day drew on,

But when the dregs of it were gone
He'd ride off to the Spaniards Inn
Where the Madeira and the din,
While damaging his ghostly liver,
Would make his affect positiver.
      The wounded hare had limped away,
It was the deep mauve time of day,
The hour of bats, and gathering gloam
That brings the bored commuter home.
He, as he gazes from the train,
At darkling, vanishing terrain,
Starts wondering what his life has meant,
A sudden, nameless discontent
Sweeps over him, and yet again
His face reflected in the pane
Becomes a mask of angst and woe…
      To get back to the story, though:
That morning, out of clean left field,
Alicia'd helpfully revealed
That she was heading North to spend
The day with an old college friend
And they were both to tag along.
The witch's will was very strong,
Come Hell or high, she'd have her way –
No one dared cross her – much less they.
To render them still more distraught
She'd asked them for a full report
Of what went on the previous night
And they'd obliged her, too, despite
The fact that nothing had occurred.
"Well, I'll be blowed! Upon my word!
You must feel marvellous! What a feat!

Young love!" she softly crooned, "How sweet!"
Causing them fretfully to bask
In the false glory of a task
Completed, that was not complete.
When they returned to her retreat
It was already dark, and there,
On the front doorstep, sat a hare.
Wounded it was, or looked to be –
Yes, it was bleeding copiously
From one front leg. "I bet it's Rick,"
The witch said. "This is rather thick,
Showing his face here after that
The other night." But there he sat,
Trembling, and gazing with sad eyes
Up at the witch, in piteous wise.
Lucy was moved, and while one can't
Be angry with a kind old aunt,
Her vengeance on her former mate
Did seem, well, disproportionate
And so she pleaded with the witch.
"Don't ask me to unpick that stitch!
His fate is fixed!" the old crone cried.
What's done is done. Suppose he died?
Who'd give a damn? He's just a hare!
You look as though you really care!
He should have thought, then, shouldn't he,
Before he went two-timing me."

      But Lucy pleaded loud and long,
Assured Alicia she'd done wrong,
And as, in your backyard, a stone,
Albeit it has never known
Any erosional mishap

Save for the dripping of a tap,
Can, merely by that dripping, be
Annihilated utterly,
So Lucy nagged and nagged, until,
At length, she'd sapped her great-aunt's will
And the old sorceress gave in.
"Oh, very well, my dear, you win,
Anything for a bit of peace,"
She grumbled, "let all rancour cease,"
And with these words she broke the spell –
Richard was back, and all was well
Save for a bandage on one foot
Where Turpin's bullet had been put.
        Such a reprieve seemed Heaven-sent –
You might think that he'd be content,
But Richard wasn't, in the least,
He hadn't been, as man or beast,
And he was not about to start:
Algie had stolen Lucy's heart;
He hadn't prized it much before
Now, filched away from him, it wore
A different look, a brighter sheen:
Envy, I guess, is what I mean,
Or vanity – yes that's the word
And ego, and the whole absurd
Macho charade that men, *tout court*,
Are so inclined to go in for.
This made him vilely out of sorts.
His mind was full of vengeful thoughts
And, in a trice, the jealous fool
Had challenged Algie to a duel!
Was he insane, or was it Fate?

"Tomorrow, Parliament Hill, at eight,
With pistols – are you up for it?"
And Algie said he was, the twit.
The pair of them were off their trees!
And as for Richard's conduct – *please!*
He'd been forgiven, but could not
Forgive in turn, the silly clot!
"Must be psychotic I suppose,
And I thought he was just morose,"
Said Lucy to herself. "Ah, well."
Then started giving Algie Hell:
"Honour and stuff – it's all old hat!"
She bellowed. "Don't be such a prat!
Tell him it's off, for Heaven's sake!
Your making a *grotesque* mistake!
Revoke… re… what's the word I want?"
But Algernon was adamant –
Honour, whatever, he must fight.

        They had a nightmare of a night.
Death's a big subject with us all –
Its charms are few, and quickly pall,
And if our lives, in some bleak place,
Connect with it, and interface,
It gnaws the psyche like a worm
Thus Algie could no more perform
Than if he had already died,
While Lucy, lying by his side,
Felt disempowered and desperate
And cursed testosterone and Fate.

        Algie got sod all sleep that night
And finally, towards first light,
Chilled to the bottom of his soul,

Opted to go out for a stroll.
It all seemed sickeningly surreal,
He felt he'd had a rotten deal.
There was no turning back, not now –
"Richard'll kill me anyhow,
Duel or no duel – go bravely, then.

He'd plumbed the Slough of Despond, when
There at his side Dick Turpin stood.
"Frettin' won't do ye any good,
He said, "you've still got time, me lad –
We've two hours – chin up! 'Tin't so bad!
Dick's goin' to teach ye 'ow to shoot."
"In two hours?!" – "Pish! Ain't nothin' to't.
'Tin't 'ard unless yer think it's 'ard.
'Ere look – ye see that there bollard?"
Some twenty, thirty yards away,
A mere shape, it being not yet day,
A bollard, stood. Dick now took aim,
The gun gave off a tongue of flame,
And in another instant they
Heard the resulting ricochet.
"There!" he observed, "'Tis easy, see?
Now let's find out 'ow good *you* be."
Turpin reloaded, cocked it, and
Placed the fine piece in Algie's hand.
"Come on, me boy – ye can but try…"
Quite how much Algie missed it by
I can't tell, though the shot was poor,
But even had it been the door
Of a proverbial barn, I fear
He'd still have gotten nowhere near.
"That maybe were a touch too 'ard.

We'll 'ead off to the Spaniards yard
And set a target up."– "Too late,"
Said Algie, "Richard's due at eight.
There's just no time." – "'Tis true, no time.
It flies so quickly it's a crime.
There's never any time," said Dick,
"Too late for ye to lean the trick.
Remember, though, to shut one eye,
Yer barrel not too low, or 'igh,
Like this, d'ye see?" He aimed again
And this time wasted a moorhen.
His face fell. "'Tis too bad, me boy.
We shall be drinkin', you 'n oi,
Up at the Spaniards Inn tonight,
And you'll be there in your own right!"
Upon which note of blunt despair
Dick Turpin vanished into air.
        Algie felt tense, and sick, and numb –
Like seeing the dentist and then some.
The sky was turning tangerine,
He bought a bun at South End Green,
And coffee in a plastic cup,
Then made his way forlornly up
Parliament Hill – the rendezvous
They'd fixed upon. "That's life for you,"
He grumbled. "Here's this gorgeous dawn,
A brand new day is being born
With hopes, and dreams, and here am I
With minutes left before I die!
I missed that bollard by a mile!"
A heron on the floating isle
Assessed him with a curious eye

As if it might be wondering why
This poor young man looked so depressed.
    Lucy turned up. She'd done her best
The night before to change his mind —
More of the same would be unkind —
She took his hand, they stood there, mum.
"And grandma...?" – "I don't think she'll come.
'It's up to him.' That's what she said.
'The boy's a fool. He's best off dead.
So he's the apple of my eye –
Tough – tell him that I said Goodbye.'"
"Yes? Witches can be odd that way.
It seems a *little* harsh, but, hey.
Is that tobacco in that tin?"
"Like one?" She rolled a fag for him.
"Hmm. This'll calm the nerves perhaps.
Today it's me on whom life craps —
I wish..."
His stomach gave a lurch.
The belfry of a nearby church
Whose name escaped him tolled the hour,
The little, cute, Rococo tower
Was glinting in the early sun.
"Here's Richard."
He was with someone.
He said: "I've brought a friend with me
To sort of act as referee
If that's OK with you." – "It's fine.
So Richard's friend marked out a line
From which they both walked fifteen paces,
As is the custom in such cases,
Then turned, and met each other's eye,

And Algie, with a Stoic sigh,
Levelled Dick's pistol, fired, and missed.
Then Richard fired, and a strange mist
Descended over Algie's eyes
And "Ah! So this is how one dies,
It's just another moment, then,
No sooner here than gone again,
As the philosophers assure us,
As one can read in Epicurus..."
Was his last thought, a learned one
Well suited to him. He was gone.

NINE

Though she would not admit the truth
Alicia'd loved the brilliant youth
But she was *Roman* in her views:
Presumably it hurt to lose
Someone she'd cared for, to the grave
Yet not one outward sign she gave
Of grief. She was as cold as ice,
And even ate an extra slice
Of buttered toast the following day
At breakfast. "It'll be OK,"
She told her sorrowful great-niece,
Life – any life – routinely sees
It's quota of calamities,
And by them it is always best
Not to be fazed, but unimpressed;
Life is a crass, insistent bore
Demanding anguish, joy, or awe –
Some strong response – at every turn –
React with total unconcern
To all its sallies – you'll implode
Unless you stick to that calm mode.
Keep punctuation spare, and stark,
Avoid the exclamation mark."
For *sangfroid* this was hard to top
And put a harsh, hard-nosed full stop
To the sad tale of Algernon —
"Why waste one's tears? What's gone is gone!"
She added, not without a wry,
Sardonic twinkle in her eye.

"He's in his grave, and furthermore
His *book* is in a bottom drawer
Which may be where the thing belongs
So there's one right to soothe our wrongs.
The critics doubtless would have panned 'im
And several trees have been left standing."
     But one exception to her cool
And, I think, admirable rule
Was Richard: she was *furious* with him –
"I was an idiot to forgive him,"
She said, "it's your fault, by the by –
Well, well, that doesn't signify,
It's too late. But he must be made
To suffer – *some* price *must* be paid.
Besides," she cried, "whatever skin
He wore he'd not be happy in.
If it's endemic, then, his pain,
Why don't I change him yet again?
This time, though, something really base,
Little, and low, and commonplace –
Which animal would suit him best?
What loathsome beast would you suggest?"
They pondered. Neither had a clue.
They spent a good hour leafing through
A book of local wildlife – bat,
Frog, ferret, squirrel, blackbird, rat,
Pike, heron, rabbit, hobby, vole –
Passed on all these, and plumped for mole.
"I'll use my strongest spell and worst!
One that can never be reversed!"
Hollered the witch, and then she spoke
Some gibberish, and a puff of smoke

Enveloped Richard where he sat
Guilt-tripping in his Camden flat.
In half a tick he had once more
Grown fur, swapped hand foot for paw,
His eyes had filled with molish tears,
New feelings, instincts, longings, fears
Welled up in him, disturbing, strange,
Marking the first phase of his change,
Man lingering, mingling with mole
Two disparate halves, one desperate whole,
Uncertain, unspecific, odd.
"Gosh, I was riled! That was a nod,"
The witch confessed, "toward somewhat
More human feelings, was it not?
Of course, emotions are mere blague
But I'll admit, I lost my rag.
I broke, for once, my Stoic rule."
"Why couldn't you have stopped the duel?"
Lucy was tempted to enquire
But thought it over, and held fire
Afraid to make this risky point
And put the fay's nose out of joint
Lest she should wind up on the Heath
With scales, or wings, or huge front teeth.
     The wise old witch was watching her...
"From your expression I infer
A question – yes, it's in your eyes."
"Well... I don't want to criticize,"
Said Lucy, "but I wonder why...
(She changed her tack) "as time went by
You couldn't have made Algernon
Less hideous? You have no son,

Which made him nigh as good as one,
You can change *your* looks, as we've seen,
In Venice." – "I know what you mean,"
Great-aunt Alicia confessed,
"Who knows? Perhaps I thought it best
For Algie to accept his lot,
To be content with what he'd got.
However, child, I must aver –
And don't be shocked at this – there were
Moments when it afforded me
A kind of pleasure, curious glee
To watch his weird and wondrous face,
Its every feature out of place,
Still struggling to be dignified
And wear its gruesomeness with pride."
    Lucy was lonely. Every day
Her aunt, worn out from witching, lay
Dead to the world upstairs, while *she*
Was left to mope, and watch TV –
Even the Guy and Gwenda Show
At ten a.m. She felt so low
She couldn't eat, or read a book,
Life gave an inch, it seemed, then took
A generous yard, if not a mile –
In this mature and maudlin style
She brooded, till it came to night
When some old film in black and white
Or promo channel brought her sleep
Neither restorative nor deep.
But, waking once at two a.m
From fitful rest, she thought of them,
The only friends she'd ever had –

Dick, with his "Pish!" and his "Egad!"
And Algie, with his dread of sex,
And brilliant brain, and inch-thick specs.
    She hit the Spaniards. They were there –
A brooding, melancholy pair
In Turpin's corner. Algernon
Was drunk. He was already on
His seventh mug of phantom beer.
Turpin stood up. "Egad, me dear!"
You'll come and join us in our nook?
'Ere's Algie, nicely pickled, look!
Don't fret! These gloomy days'll pass.
Man that is born of woman, lass,
'E cometh up, and… 'ow's it go?
This cursed mem'ry, I don't know!
Anyroad, like the grass 'e's mown.
Ale for the lady! Sit ye down."
She sat, and drank, and was, quite soon,
Not over the proverbial moon
But certainly not under it.
Algie looked bear-gnawn, canker-bit
(In other words, the worse for wear)
He sat, with a self-pitying air,
Brooding on all the years he'd missed.
He glared at her and shook his fist –
"It's your fault! Yours alone!" he said,
"My curtailed life is on your head!"
Because of you I'm now a ghost
Left here to brood on chances lost,
The mark I'd meant to make, unmade.
I'd have done great things, had I stayed –
My book was brilliant, a gem –

I would have shown the lot of them
Instead of which I'm in an inn
Getting rat-arsed with Dick Turpin.
Fame, riches, honour, all that shit –
I should have had my share of it
Driven fast cars, pulled chicks, walked tall –
And thanks to you I missed it all!
You've well and truly buggered me!
I hate you. HATE. H A T E!"
"That's not you talking, it's the beer,"
Said Lucy softly, "calm down, dear,
You may say something you'll regret,
I tried to stop you, don't forget."
"The lass is right," said Dick, "cool down,
I was the talk, once, of the town,
Much good it did me. Leave 'er be
'N 'ave another ale, on me."
"What would you know about it? Eh?"
Said Algie shrilly. "You're OK –
You may be dead, but you've got fame –
All round the globe they know your name."
"Ay, up and down, and to and from,
I's even got me own dot com!"
Dick boasted.
Drink, I must address
You now: I love you, more or less –
To You all reverence is due,
Whatever name we give to you –
Yasigi, Dionysus, Sura,
If care's a sickness, you're its curer –
I love you, as I think I said,
Whether you're brown, gold, white or red,

Not when I wake up overhung
With foul breath and a furry tongue,
But overall, and on the whole,
As when you lubricate the soul,
Inspire the mind, calm quarrels down,
Give us a *boldness* we'd not known.
　　　Lucy grew bold. Perhaps to hurt
Poor Algie, she began to flirt,
Like a young serving-wench, with Dick.
Though rough in some ways, Dick was slick
With women, and, in his short life,
Having steered well clear of a wife,
He'd satisfied an itchy crotch
Till his bedpost was one big notch.
He had a winsome way with him
And now, but merely on a whim,
While circling her with a huge arm,
Zapped Lucy with his lethal charm.
Soon she was sitting on his knee
While as for poor old Algie, he
Began to feel the deadly chill
Of seeing someone you love thrill
To someone else's talk, and touch –
Plus he was dead – it was too much.
As Turpin wooed and Lucy swooned
Each word they uttered dealt a wound
To Algie's soul. "The bitch! The tart!"
He muttered, with a broken heart.
　　　"Well, old Dick's tired, me lad, my sweet,"
Said Turpin, rising to his feet.
"'Tis late. I'm trottin' off upstairs.
I'll drain me drink to drown me cares

And take a gracious leave o' you."
Then Lucy said: "May I come too?"
As though she'd been a leaf, or feather,
Dick caught her up and off together
This pair of one-night-standers went
While leaving Algie, discontent
Personified, to quaff his beer
And wish that he might disappear.
His ego had been torn to tatters
(Egos tear worst in sexual matters.)
    Dick's was the best and biggest room.
The dim light of a crescent moon
Was slanting in through shutter-slats
Revealing his three cornered hats,
Boots, great coat, pistols, and shot-gun,
A portrait, too, superbly done
By Romney, of old Dick himself,
Propped casually on the mantelshelf.
"Be it yer first time, wench?" he said,
"Ah, well – 'tis nothin' ye need dread."
 He laid her gently on the bed
And sat beside her. "Yare, I am,
And I'll be gentle as a lamb,
Not Dick as all the world once feared!"
    He wasn't lying. It appeared
That underneath that frightening frame,
Behind the Dick of darker fame,
The terror of the King's highway,
A different man, a sweet one, lay.
He took her in his arms. Soon, she
Was in the sky, or was it sea?
A flying, floating, falling sense,

Flowing from Lord alone knew whence,
Engulfing her, the room, the world –
Everything opened, and unfurled,
Went out, sublimely, on a limb.
He undressed her, she undressed him,
The furnaces of lust were fanned,
Electric currents from his hand
Went sizzling through her – he had lit
Her fuse, had put a flame to it
That burned at a delicious rate
And threatened soon to detonate
In an immense explosion.
But,
Like a director'd shouted "Cut!",
He stopped dead. "Turpin, shame on thee!
Lord, what a drunken fool ye be!
God dash and darn ye, man!" Dick cried,
"Why, if yer's not all boozifoied,
Yer silly, bibbin' nincompoop,
You've gone 'n got Madeira droop!"
"What's up?" "What's *down*, ye mean! 'Twon't rise –
Me cursed yardarm, damn its eyes!"
Damn the Madeira! Damn it all!
'Tis danglin', look, beyond recall!"
"Oh, dear! I see now what you mean!"
For, like a shrivelled runner bean,
His barely visible manhood,
The same one that had stoutly stood
For many an English wench before,
Was hanging down, and yet once more
Lucy was thwarted. "Not *again!*"
She muttered, "God Almighty! MEN!"

That's it! My maidenhead can stay!
Virginity, you rule, OK!"
Their parting was a frosty one.
"But you'll forgive me when I'm gone
For you'll not see me any more…"
Said Turpin, as she slammed the door.
　　As she was walking home, distraught,
She had a sudden afterthought:
In her obsession with his ****
She hadn't said a word to Dick
About the antidote, and now
It was too late: they'd had a row,
Were never going to meet again,
Or that's what he'd implied just then.
Why was she so obsessed with bed?
She could have had the loot instead.
"Tonight's been a catastrophe!
Is someone up there mad at me?
No, no – I mustn't rail at Fate."
(She'd reached Alicia's front gate)
"There isn't any Grand Design –
We make our own luck, I've made mine,
And shit-poor luck it's proved to be –
I'll get me to a nunnery!"

TEN

"One thing still niggles me, you know,"
The witch, in tones of almost woe,
Announced to Lucy one fine day
When summer fairly blazed away,
Breaking its usual, pluvial norm,
The Heath was dotted with the form
Of many a near-nude girl and boy
Filling the voyeur's heart with joy,
And a pot-bellied bullfinch sang
In every bush; when church-bells rang
The lazy hours redundantly
Since people had no place to be
Other than where they were; and when,
From about noon till five p.m.,
The air was thick with haze and heat,
The witch announced, and I repeat:
"One thing still niggles me, you know,
And you too, or it should do so:
That pile of gold you never got,
Still lurking in some unknown spot,"
Thus spoke, provokingly, the witch.
"Tell me about it! Life's a bitch!"
Said Lucy.
Later on that day
As, soaking up the sun, she lay
In a spot near the old stock-pond
Of which she was especially fond,
A *mole* came up and said hello,
Nuzzling her leg to let her know

That it was there. At once she guessed
That this was Richard. She expressed
No pity this time, was, in fact,
Almost inclined towards an act
Of vengeance, such as squashing him.
Then she reflected on how grim
His current, moly life must be –
"And serve him damned well right!" thought she,
"Leave him alone and let him stew."
And so she simply shouted: "Shoo!
Piss off! Don't spoil my afternoon!"
And Richard scuttled off.
                                    But soon
Determination brought him back –
Let her get mad, he'd take the flack,
Even if squashing should ensue.
This obstinate approach was due
To an instinctive attitude
With which all talpids are imbued,
Who, on a scale of one to ten,
Score equal top with mules and men
For pointless, stupid stubbornness.

       Richard had felt a vague distress –
I won't say penitence as such,
For a mole's heart is hard to touch,
But some small smidgen of regret
(He wasn't *wholly* mole quite yet)
At having been the tragic cause
Of Algie's reaching Stygian shores
Far sooner than he should have done.
"How," he reflected, "to atone?"
And then, one fateful morning, he

Was digging out his gallery,
Progressing yard by gruelling yard,
When, after several hours of hard,
Claw-blunting burrowing, he found
A chest, some two feet underground.
He gnawed its lid all afternoon
Till finally a gold doubloon
Appeared in the resulting gap –
He'd found Dick Turpin's hoard, poor chap.
While some pretend that money's dross –
(Till they experience its loss)
Richard was wise, and knew its worth,
And, having managed to unearth
This stash of loot, he also knew
Just who he ought to give it to.
He'd actually been on his way
To Lucy's home, when, there she lay,
As she'd been doing all day long,
In nothing but a bra and thong,
A sad reminder of the cost
Of his rash act, in pleasures lost.
      He motioned to her with a paw
To follow. "What's he beckoning for?"
She thought. "Well, what have I to lose?"
She donned her T-shirt, jeans and shoes,
And off he shot, snout down, eyes low,
Across the Heath, with her in tow.
A mole can move at quite a pace
And pretty soon they'd reached his place
(Which lay a little way beyond
The Kenwood Ladies' Bathing Pond).
A raised paw bade her wait, then he

Dove down into his gallery,
She waited, baffled, but quite soon
Richard came back with a doubloon
Between his teeth. At once she knew
What all this had been leading to –
That buried here lay Turpin's loot,
Richard, the wretch, had led her to it,
Atonement had, in part, been made.

She came back later with a spade
And disinterred Dick's treasure chest.
She felt, it must be said, quite blessed
To have this windfall come her way:
No matter what Saint Paul* may say
In life it doesn't go amiss
To have some cash – as much as this
Might be to take it to excess
But *some*, at any rate – oh, yes:
If life's a road and we're a car
Then wonga, dosh, spondulicks are,
If not the gas, the engine oil –
They minimise our toil and moil.

Richard was feeling good inside,
His conscience had been mollified,
Even his new and bestial form
Ceased to distress him, as a warm,
Soft, balmy sunset rose to don
Its orange coat, and dusk drew on.
"I'll never buy it heart and soul
But it's not so bad being a mole,"
He thought, "and after all, I asked

---

*First Epistle to Timothy: "Money is the root of all evil."

For this grim plight."
But as he basked
In such reflections, from the sky
A kestrel had him in her eye.
Still hungry, hunting, hovering
Despite a long day on the wing,
She was relieved to chance at last
On this quite choice, if small, repast...
She stooped, dropped on it like a stone,
And made the meagre prey her own.

ELEVEN

Aahh, shucks,
Everything's in a state of flux.
— Heraclitus

God (or the Devil) only knows
Why, after brief thought, Lucy chose
To give the treasure to her aunt.
For safekeeping. We sometimes can't
Accommodate good luck, I guess,
It doesn't seem to coalesce
With life as it's so far been led –
We should be chuffed, but are, instead,
Chary. She couldn't have done worse:
"Count" Cagliostro'd placed a curse
Upon the loot, in vengeful spite
For being conned at cards that night
In Venice. Quite some hex he'd cast:
Into whoever's hands it passed,
Be they mere mortal, mighty fay,
Warlock, or witch, or wizard, they
Must die. No magic could avert
Their doom. (Shit happens when you hurt
The pride of that particular race –
They will not suffer loss of face.)
      "Why, thank you, dear!" the sorceress said –
Perhaps she'd steered things, not been led,
Tired of her life's unending game
She'd seized this one chance, when it came,
Of finally rising from the table –

Would have before, had she been able.
Weary or not, that night she died,
Presumably well satisfied
With having seen nine centuries.
Her valedictory words were these:
"I think the custom, when one dies,
Is to be witty, or advise,
One or the other. Well, if so,
I choose the latter – here we go:
The nothingness of scorn and noise
Awaits you, child – not merely boys –
Restrict your wishes – if you do
Life has more chance of pleasing you;
Lend no one money, not unless
Its loss won't leave you in a mess;
It's no use taking exercise –
However fit one is, one dies;
Dieting should be shunned, likewise:
I've eaten what the Hell I chose
Since I was in my baby clothes
And I'm eight hundred and nineteen!
Make sure your ears are always clean;
Avoid three people out of four –
One will be dangerous, one a bore,
One feathering his or her own nest.
I'm sorry, I forget the rest.
My dearest wish, my fondest dream,
My whole life's holy grail has been
Simply to breathe the perfect breath –
I never did, and now here's death!"
     I'd like to say there was a break
In the fine weather, for the sake

Of marking aunt Alicia's loss
But Nature didn't give a toss
Or feel the tiniest bit bereft –
Something would fill the gap she'd left.
Aunt Sybil, though, did seem to care,
Bestrode her broomstick to be there.
The funeral was a quiet one –
Vicar, butler, Lucy, crone
And cat comprised the whole affair
In that enchanting Georgian square
Church Row, in Saint John's parish church.
"She finally fell off her perch,
The crazy, mischievous old crow!"
Aunt Sibyl said. "Well, there you go,
Death knocks on every blessed door,
Doubtless it won't be long before
He even comes and knocks on mine –
'Hurry up, please!' he'll say, 'It's time!'
Well, who knows? Maybe I'll be out
And so escape the general rout!
Oh, either way, one mustn't moan."
        Lucy was totally alone.
Where could virginity and death
Be better coped with than the Heath –
A good, long, life-affirming stroll
To mend the mind and soothe the soul.
She climbed to Parliament Hill-top,
Reaching a temporary stop
To take in Wednesday afternoon.
A prancing kite, a proud balloon
Made pastel patches in the air.
Was there a POINT, like them, somewhere

Suspended? What that point might be
It's not permitted us to see
The trick of it is not to mind –
Accept that, thus far, we are blind
And imitate the calm tick-tock
And tranquil motion of a clock,
Unthinking, regular, and slow –
Like Epicurus, was it? No...

    Here, Highgate Hill, a fine backdrop,
Old mansions clambering, at the top
Saint Michael's' slim and soaring spire
Pricking the bums of the Heavenly choir,
Gothically glorious when the light
'S caught it, as it had now, just right.
She buttoned up her overcoat.
A lonely (and illegal) boat
Whizzed round the model-boating pond –
Whose surface, at this hour, had donned
A cloak of dancing light, as though
A Monet, or a Pissarro
Had come to life. Just one or two
Couples – enough to gladden you
But not so many as to cause ya
An overwhelming sense of nausea.
She watched the hi-tech toy go round
And, in its futile motion, found
Something – perhaps a metaphor
For what she dimly sensed, not saw:
Restrict your wants, the witch had said,
Forge, circumspectly, straight ahead –
Maybe she'd meant it would be best
To give up her obsessive quest –

If no man came, then be content
With her absurd predicament -
Or might there be a happy mean?
A proper, prudent in-between?
Mimic, don't try to *be*, the tiger –
Attempt some hills, but not the Eiger.
The pond, with its insistent sheen,
A dome, once copper, now bright green,
Woods waving in the wind, that spire,
Above her, looking even higher –
Sensory overload had come –
Mission accomplished, head for home.

*

"There's someone on the telephone,
A Mr Mungo, Miss."
"Mungo!"
"Hello, dear heart! Hello! Hell-oooo!
Long time no speak, and all that rot.
All right?"
"Not really… No! I'm not!"
"Oh, come along! For Heaven's sake,
Cheer *uuuuup!* I know! We'll have a wake!
A joint one – grand-mother and -son.
What say you? Are you up for one?
Luce? Are you there?"
"All right, then, fine."
"Wicked!" he squealed. "Your place or mine?"

*

The butler has brought down a book.
"The mistress wanted you to look
At this, Miss, if you'd care to." – "Yes!
I would! Good! Splendid!" Lucy says

And, opening the volume, sees
The following on its frontispiece:
Spells, Magic Ones Or Otherwise
Depending, Mainly, On Who Tries.
"I wonder, will it work for me?"
Thinks Lucy. "Might as well just see…
'To turn a toad into a cat
Or vice versa' – let's try that."
She speaks the spell. "Well, I'll be blowed!"
The cat has vanished, and a toad
Is squatting in its place. "Whey hey!"
She speaks the spell the other way
Which puts the cat back on its chair –
He crouches, scowling at her, there.
She spends the next few happy hours
In playing with her new-found powers
Which proves the perfect way to make
The time pass, prior to the wake.

*

Later, the wake is in full swing,
The mansion fairly quivering
With music, dancing, mindless chat,
Quick shags in corners, all of that,
As Lucy's friends and Mungo's mix
And spliff and snort and get their kicks
In the erotically charged gloom
Of many a mock-Medieval room.
A thought has entered Lucy's head:
Might Mungo stand her in some stead?
Apart from being oddly-sexed
He fits the bill in most respects,
Is even handsome, when the light

Is either off, or not too bright,
He *might* be suited the task...
There's just one problem – she daren't ask,
Or hasn't plucked up courage yet. He
Is holding forth about Rossetti,
Saying things never said before,
People are listening in awe.
"Mungo... I was just wondering if..."
She interrupts, but, loath to miff
Her new-found, brilliant friend, breaks off
With nothing but a nervous cough.
Much later they're alone. She's coy
Now that at last she has the boy
All to herself. She takes his hand,
She tentatively strokes it, and
Tries to convey she's easy meat.
Says Mungo: "Spit it out, my sweet:
What do you want? No, let me guess –
You want to fuck me." – "Erm... Well... Yes!"
Says Lucy. "You're a virgin... well?"
"Hey! How, by all the fiends in Hell,
Did you know that?" – "It's plain as *day!*"
He countered, to her huge dismay.
She was abashed, and riled to boot -
"I've worn it, then, like some loud suit,
This wretched innocence of mine!
Oh, well, I've laid it on the line."
She laughs it off: "So – what d'you say?"
"It isn't *quite* my *bag*, but hey,
No harm in giving it a try.
Might even like it... pigs might fly.
And if it doesn't work, who cares?"

"Alright, then, shall we go upstairs?"
"Yo, sister! Bust my goddam bones!"
He cries, in unconvincing tones,
"Ignite my fire – *if* there's a fire."
And on that note the pair retire.

TWELVE

"I'm sorry, sweetie," Mungo sighed,
"Believe you me, I really tried."
(This as they breakfasted next day)
"Tried?! God knows why I had to! Hey,
You've got a *gorgeous* bod, *and* face,
But shagging's just so... *commonplace,*
And *dirty,* too, you must admit –
I'll *never* get a taste for it.
I procreate a different way –
No, darling, *je suis désolé*
But hairy crannies, sweaty nooks
Are simply *not* where Mungo looks
For his posterity, or kicks,
Art is my thing: a daily fix
Of *culture* keeps me very happy -
I fear I'll never change a nappy
Nor any seed of mine be sown
Yet from me *something* will have grown –
That might sound like a precious pose
But *Art's* my sex, my offspring, shows.
"No worries, dear, that's fine by me.
Oh, sod it, pass the F-ing tea,"
Said Lucy, "I shall crack this yet."
"Yees, that's the spirit, Luce my pet –
What are you? Not yet twenty-one.
Just you keep calm and carry on.
You bide your time and it'll come
Or rather, go. It's troublesome,
It needn't drive you up the wall,

You'll be invited to the ball,
(Pardon the accidental pun)
You'll soon be having *heaps* of fun.
Sex isn't everything – is it?
Well, if it is, *I'm* in deep shit!"
    Now she could visit any place,
Had the whole run of time and space,
She fell to wondering where to go.
Rome in the time of Cicero
Was what, at length, she settled on
(She'd just been reading *Rubicon*)
An era, as, from school, she knew
When virgins had their value too,
Nay, were, if anything, revered,
Not seen as something somewhat weird.
They tended Vesta's sacred fire,
The welfare of the whole Empire
Would be in very serious doubt
If that flame ever should go out
So hand-picked virgins, day and night,
Stood vigil, keeping it alight;
It was an honour to be chosen
Although their sex-lives thus were frozen.
"To meet those women – might it not...
I don't know, maybe this is rot,
But their advice could help me cope
With my predicament." This hope
Brightened her mood. "First rate idea!"
She hurtled through the stratosphere
Astride the besom's sturdy pole,
And in two hours she'd reached her goal –
The slender columns, in a ring,

As elegant as anything,
That are unique to Vesta's fane,
Or temple. There her magic plane
She parked, and on the great oak door
Knocked thrice.
It wasn't long before
A woman answered Lucy's knock,
A giant Juno, with a shock
Of unkempt, Amazonian hair
And such a disconcerting air
As all (or men, at least) must fear –
Half Kirsty Wark, half Germaine Greer.
  "What have you come about?" she cried,
"Chaste, are you?" – "And how!" – "Step inside
Before the wind blows out the flame
The Senate fines my ass again
And I get thrown out on the street.
You look perturbed. What's wrong, my sweet?
I won't bite. Come in, shut the door.
Now, then, what can I do you for?
You're not tomorrow's sacrifice?"
"I came to ask you some advice."
"Splendid! Advice is my forte.
Sit down, my dear, and fire away.
Whatever problem, I'm shit-hot.
Falernian? It's all I've got."
(She poured her guest a glass of wine.)
"I'm listening. Lay it on the line."
"Well, something's really bugging me,"
Lucy began. "Virginity.
I try to shake it off, it sticks.
I've got myself into a fix.

I met four likely-seeming men,
One less so, bedded each of them,
Each time I thought I'd made it, but,
At the last moment, things went phut!
So what I need to know is this:
Ought I take it so amiss?
Is life without sex just not on
Or oughtn't it to trouble one?
As Vesta's priestess, you should know.
What must I do? Go with the flow?
Resist frustration? Hang in there?
Because right now I'm going spare."
"No," said the priestess with a sigh,
"You *should* be pissed off, and here's why:
If this world were a chariot
It'd need two wheels, would it not?
We have two eyes, walk on two legs,
For breakfast we have two fried eggs –
Well, when I'm hungry I have three
But anyway you follow me –
All human life is *binary*
And nowhere more so than perhaps
With sex: the fact is, girls need chaps
And chaps need girls. The stuff of life
It is, it's everywhere, it's rife,
In town and country, shack and court
Couples canoodle and cavort,
The world's a *maelstrom* of desire,
It's burning, just like Vesta's fire,
For ever and ever, night and day;
Without some action to allay
Its frazzling, *humungous* heat

And briefly make the flames retreat,
The conflagration grows and grows
Till some internal gasket blows
And, ten to one, you go insane
As I have, in this cursed fane.
Just look around the world – you'll see
That Nature's at it, constantly:
The beasts that crawl upon the earth
Shag, ball and bonk for all they're worth,
The fowls that flutter in the air
Do little else that I'm aware,
And fish, down in the deep blue sea,
Are as up for it as fish can be;
Sparrows and pigeons, goats and sheep
Do three things: **** and eat and sleep,
No creature can get by without it,
You're *bound* to be hung up about it!
I've sat here tending Vesta's flame,
Oo, since the Carthaginians came –
It feels that long at any rate –
I'm guardian of my country's fate
But am I *happy?* Am I heck!
Look at me! I'm a nervous wreck!
All Vesta's priestesses are wrecks
And why? Because we get no sex!"

    Lucy was desolated by
The mad old priestess's reply –
She'd hoped to be consoled, instead
Bleak thoughts were swirling round her head.
Of course she couldn't leave without
Taking a little peek about
A city only she'd have seen

Not tumbled down, but all pristine,
Not grey with age, but polished white
And gleaming in the sun's last light.
She started at the Palatine
The Mayfair, Knightsbridge, of its time,
A splendid complex of first rate
Late pre-imperial real estate.
For this, then, making a bee-line
She came upon a specially fine
And spacious palace – one of those
With colonnades and porticoes
And pools and peristyles, that will
Pop up in movies by De Mille
(Fredrick March might be living there,
Charles Laughton, or Claudette Colbert).
    As Lucy left her broom before
The entrance, on an upper floor
A man came out to take a gander
At the fab view from his veranda.
Quite short he was, with close-cropped hair,
His tunic left his strong limbs bare,
His eyes were shrewd, his bearing regal,
He had the hooter of an eagle,
And, though he was quite simply clad,
The garment he was wearing had,
Right down the front, a purple band
To let the punters understand
That here was someone pretty grand,
Perhaps the man himself, no less –
Caesar, or such was Lucy's guess.
Almost at once his piercing eyes
Lighted on Lucy's naked thighs

(For she had on the mini bought
In Camden Lock). At first he thought
She was a slave-girl, but her look
Had something in it that he took
To indicate a higher class.
A Caesar doesn't *make* a pass –
He drew her to him with his eye,
Then shouted: *"Ave!"* (which means "Hi!"
In Latin). A lubricious look
Was followed by a *"Veni huc!"*
("Come here!") *"Huc veni, o puella!*
And that was all he had to tell her.
Her Latin being excellent
She understood, and up she went,
Ascending by a marble stair.
She knew him. In her brain somewhere
She had his features stowed away.
To end all doubt, he said: "salve!
Sum Iulius Caesar. Quis es tu?"
("I'm Julius Caesar. Who are you?")
"Cenabo mox." ("It's supper time.")
"Visne cenare?" ("Care to dine?)
      They dined on classic Roman fare –
Thrushes, a turbot and a hare.
Caesar held forth, his silver tongue
Wooing the charming, nubile young
Creature who'd dropped into his lap
With all the cunning of a chap
Who's knocked about and knows the world.
Her toes, beneath the table, curled
With admiration, pleasure, lust –
He was the best one yet, a must!

No reason, really, was required
Why Caesar should be so desired:
He being possessed of, inter alia,
Two arms, two legs, and genitalia,
Which, for a girl so long denied,
Rendered him amply qualified.
But, to augment these properties,
He was a great man, if you please,
One of the greatest of all time,
The victim of a famous crime,
And powerful, which, in men, can pack
A hefty aphrodisiac:
So often we see women swoon
Over an ugly, fat tycoon,
Bald minister, clapped-out rock star,
Merely by dint of who they are,
But someone with his face on coins…
     For his part, Lucy'd stirred his loins
And, seeing her intelligence,
He had the artfulness and sense
To treat her as an equal – aired
Most complex issues, freely shared
His worries with her – plans for war,
Reforms that he was striving for,
Alliances, cabals and coups,
Till Lucy had begun to lose
Her patience: "That's all well and good,
No need to overegg the pud',"
She thought, "some *action's* what we need –
You're famed for that, now do the deed!"
He read this message in her eye
And placed a soft hand on her thigh:

"Mox futuam te," he now said,
("Don't fret, we'll soon be going to bed.")
But added he could not that night
And would tomorrow be all right?
Tonight he'd too much work to do,
The following morning he was due
In Senate. If she could but see
The mountains of petitions he
Must read, and he'd a speech to write –
If she could just wait this one night
Tomorrow he could guarantee
Patience rewarded – generously.

    She had no choice. It was agreed.
When she awoke next morning, he'd
Already set off for the Forum.
The palace had its proper quorum
Of people bustling to and fro
And Lucy watched them come and go
With fascination, and eavesdropped
As news was told and gossip swapped.
One fellow harped about the date:
    "Well, it's the Ides of March then, mate,"
This man remarked to one confrère,
"Today, in case you're not aware,
Caesar's been warned to mind his arse
'Coz something dire could come to pass."
The Ides of March! Then could this be
March Fifteenth, Forty-Four B.C.,
The day when Caesar met his end,
Topped, by his best, most trusted friend?
She *had* to save him. In no time
She'd hurried down the Palatine

And reached the Forum's bustling streets.
The kind of chaos that one meets
In London, any working day
Was not a patch on this mêlée –
She fought to move from hereon in,
The place was in a manic spin –
Slaves, lawyers, prostitutes, street urchins,
Clerks, senators, shopkeepers, merchants
Milling and muddling along,
The weak being jostled by the strong,
The fast expleting at the slow…
She almost made it even so,
She ran into the Senate just
As Brutus grit his teeth and thrust
His dagger in his old friend's flank –
In went the blade, down Caesar sank,
Eyes filmed with death, and as he died
"Vale, Lucia!" Caesar cried
("Lucy, farewell!") (He *didn't* say,
As myth reports: *"Et tu, Brute!"*)

*

"I'm fed up! This whole business stinks!
It has to be a curse, a jinx!
That's three guys dead, as a result
Of dating this one-girl death-cult!"
Sulked Lucy that same afternoon
As she flew homewards, plunged in gloom.
"Well, as of now, the project's canned –
I'm simply going to have to stand
Being less worldly than my peers
If I remain that way for years.

To force things is to go against
Nature, or so, at last, I've sensed.
A book, and glass of Waitrose red,
Will have to do, for now, in bed."
    The sun had set upon a Heath
Dick's loot no longer lurked beneath;
A kestrel pellet lay out there,
Abandoned and forgotten, where,
Only last week, a mole had been;
Turpin was at the Spaniards Inn
And Algie sitting next to him,
Wishing they were discussing art
Not who could do the loudest fart;
Great-aunt Alicia was gone,
Yet, notwithstanding, carried on –
The erstwhile twinkle in her eye
Was lighting up the Hampstead sky.

THE END

RANJIT BOLT is one of the world's leading translators and adaptors for the stage. His adaptation of Corneille's comedy *Le Menteur* was performed at London's Old Vic Theatre (1989) in an acclaimed production directed by Jonathan Miller. A long collaboration with iconic director Sir Peter Hall followed, as well as productions at the National Theatre and the RSC. Bolt was awarded an OBE in 2003 for services to literature. His translation of *Cyrano de Bergerac* was staged at the Roundabout Theatre on Broadway in New York in 2012. *Losing It* is his first novel.

RODDY MAUDE-ROXBY has illustrated Mike Dibb's *Spellwell* (Muswell Press, 2010) and Jonas Cleary's *Brothers, Sisters... The Trilogy* (Mammas Mammon, 2010). Maude-Roxby is also a well-known actor who has worked with Mark Rylance, Alan Bennett, Peter Cook, Peter Brook, Jonathan Miller, Spike Milligan and N.F. Simpson.